HOW TO ENLIST THE POWER OF GOD
TO HEAL YOUR HURT, RESTORE YOUR JOY,
AND GUARANTEE YOUR VICTORY
IN THE BATTLES OF LIFE

H.B. BENDER

Jesus, The Greatest Warrior

ISBN 978-0-9842576-0-7

Dedication

To my brother, who daily picks himself up and gets back in the fight. Keep the faith, my brother; God is not through with you yet.

And to my children. I want so much more for you. Trust Jesus with all your heart and obey all His commands that it may go well with you. I wish I had been better for you, but, "although I can't be all you need, I know there's one who can. He'll gladly be what you need, just bow your head and fold your hands. I'll pray you're always in His care and trust your lives to Him… Just know in my heart that I can't wait, till I can be your daddy again."

Acknowledgments

So many people have played a role leading up to this point. I will begin with Chaplain Michael Zell, who took a weeping initial-entry-training Soldier under his wing and encouraged me to pursue my calling in ministry as a chaplain.

To the Rader and McDonald families, who adopted me in Texas and were "Jesus with skin on," ministering to me and my children during the toughest part of my life.

Josh, Amy, Zack, Tom, Amy, Bob, June, Liz, Suzy, Ian and Terry… your kindness will never be justly recompensed this side of glory. Thank you.

Bob and June, I am so grateful for your loving encouragement and careful review of this project. Your editing made this book "much more better."

And Marcia Ford. You are the *Dr. Pepper* of book doctors. In Texas, that is quite a compliment. Your insight added clarity and flow to the manuscript.

Carolyn Farino, I'm so fortunate to have your talent on this project. You are without a doubt, "NFL" as my XO used to say. Thanks for helping me make this book and web-site "NFL" as well.

Jeff Fatherree, you are a marketing master. I'm so appreciative for your input, guidance and example of perseverance. Best of luck with www.getromeonow.com – I know it will be a huge success.

Of course, I am indebted to the "Swine Master," Zach Johnson and his lovely wife, and my friend, Shannon Johnson for their friendship and support. You two are a gift from heaven, for which I am both blessed and grateful.

Speaking of gifts, I would be remiss not to express gratitude for the treasure of my parents. What good fortune to have been raised by the two of you. Dad, you taught me fairness, justice, forgiveness, compassion for the less fortunate, hard work, unswerving faith, and irrepressible optimism in the face of misfortune. Mom, I fall so short of your example of sacrifice, submission to God's authority, servanthood, selfless generosity, prayer, worship, and love for Jesus expressed in personal evangelism. I want to be just like you when I grow up.

Grandma, thank you for showing me that Jesus is all we need in life. You model that better than anyone I know.

And to Jesus, this entire book is an acknowledgment.

Foreward

If you are battling discouragement, disappointment, or depression resulting from broken relationships, broken dreams, or broken health, turn the fight of your life over to Jesus, the Greatest Warrior, who...

Will always place the mission of saving you first,
Will never leave you in your fallen condition,
Will never quit you, and
Will never accept defeat for you

...but will instead turn your battles into blessings, your tragedy into triumph, your heartache into happiness, your panic into peace, your sorrow into song, and transform you from victim into victor!

Table of Contents

Introduction

Life is a battle. It would be nice if battles were restricted to those in the military, but they are not. Perhaps you are in the midst of a great battle right now. Are you fighting to save your marriage? Struggling to keep your family together? Battling for your economic survival? Maybe you are countering enemies at work who are gunning for your position or seeking to do you in? Competing for a job? Perhaps you are staving off another round of loneliness, grief, overwhelming sadness, or depression? Fighting for your very life against some sickness or disease? Battling to keep hope alive, to keep your dreams alive?

I wonder if we share the same experience. It seems as

if I've spent my entire existence rowing my small boat over the turbulent seas of life, trying to get to the shores of the ideal. Shores where the promise of a happy family life, good health, positive self-image, job satisfaction, financial security, and social status all await me—mine for the taking, if I could just get to those blasted shores.

So I press on, straining at those oars with every ounce of strength I can muster in a futile effort to overcome the tide and the wind and the waves that, in concert, all seem to conspire against me to keep me from that ideal existence I so desire. And just when I seem to be within reach of my dreams and all of my hard work and sacrifice seem to be paying off, a low, rumbling noise off in the distance catches my attention. I turn my head only to be greeted with the frightful vision of yet another tidal wave of unforeseen circumstances rising toward me in a great wall of irreversible force to sweep me away from what I was so close to attaining, what I so desperately long for, what I have worked so hard to reach. Taking one last glance toward the shores of my dreams, I get swept away by the rushing waters of circumstance. No matter how I struggle against those rapids or how strenuously I reach for those fading shores in the hopes that someone would grasp my hand or throw me a line to pull me to safety, those foaming, roaring waters of unfavorable circumstance just keep carrying me farther and farther away from where I want to be. In one last-ditch effort, I grasp desperately at the first substitute that floats by in a vain attempt to keep from drowning in despair. Clinging to it fiercely, I pray that it will keep me afloat and that it will provide a sense of stability in these turbulent times and restore my hope—the hope of returning to what I once knew before these traumatic events ripped me away from my normal life.

Eventually, however, this false life preserver fails, and as reality dashes my dreams once again, the distorted, grief-stricken look on my face outwardly reveals the despair and disappointment I feel inwardly as I dejectedly surrender to these circumstances, these forces, these waters beyond my control. Waters that drag me relentlessly downstream, plunging me to the depths of depression, dragging me along the very rock bottom of life as the rest of the world rushes over in a torrent.

Melodramatic? Perhaps. But that is how I often feel. Have you ever reached a point where life has beaten the dreams out of you? Has life ever knocked you flat on your back, leaving you with nowhere to look but up? Have you ever, out of sheer depression, wanted to just close your eyes, never to open them again, because you don't want to see where you have been knocked down from or be reminded of all that you've lost? Ever wanted to just give up the fight? Quit the battle?

Maybe you're reading this book after having received devastating news from your doctor. The tests have come back positive. You have a terminal illness or a disease known for its long, painful treatment. In an instant, your future is now and forever altered. Denial is the first response. "No! This is not happening to me! This can't happen to me! Why me? Why now? This can't be happening to me now!" Denial, however, soon gives way to your greatest fear, and now all you want to do is close your eyes to hide from that fear.

A fate just as bad occurs when you have to watch someone close to you endure sickness, injury, or disease. Few things are harder than seeing someone you love writhing in agony or attached to IVs, feeding tubes, and ventilators, as you stand by, completely helpless to alleviate their suffering. Love is always willing to bear the pain and misery of another. In that moment of helplessness, there is a great temptation to

shake your fists toward the heavens and cry out, "God, I would do anything, and I would give anything to stop their pain, but I don't know how, nor do I have the power! Yet You, who claim to have all knowledge and all power and all goodness, You who could stop their pain, seem to just sit there in the heavens doing nothing! Why, God?" During those times it seems as though He doesn't know how to heal, knows how but lacks the power to heal or, worse yet, knows how and has the power but doesn't care enough to heal.

These questions are especially poignant when children suffer. It is a terrible thing to see little ones endure agony. Children should never have to wear hospital gowns or walk around with IVs stuck in their arms. Their little lives are supposed to be filled with joy and play and fun, not sickness and treatments and therapy. These are times when you might most want to close your eyes to block out the vision of others in misery.

Maybe you want to close your eyes, not to shut out visions of others enduring misery, but to avoid visions of others enjoying the happiness life has cruelly denied you. You see couples walking hand-in-hand, looking deeply and longingly into each other's eyes, and you long for that type of intimacy with someone, someone who can wash away the intense loneliness you feel in your heart. Maybe you see a little girl hug her daddy's neck in the mall or a father and son bonding while playing catch in the park, and these visions trigger a great emotional pain that wells up from deep within you, erupting in a flood of tears as you fight to regain composure while resenting the fact that you have been robbed of such cherished moments. The half-eaten fries and one-legged, half-dressed Barbie dolls littering the back seat of your car that used to be so annoying are now priceless remnants of a lost treasure whose absence causes deep, heartfelt grief. While driving, perhaps you look through the rearview mirror into the back seat, and there you see what your heart feels. Emptiness. What you wouldn't give to once again have the tops of disheveled blond heads bobbing around in that rearview mirror. What you wouldn't give to hear the laughter, the singing, or the ceaseless questions of restless children in that backseat. At this moment, even their incessant arguing would be a sweet and joyful sound to your aching, lonely heart.

Perhaps there are those reading this book who at one point had almost given up on finding that "significant other" when, out of nowhere, like an unexpected gift, that soul mate you had been longing for walked into

your life. Up to that point, you didn't even realize how empty and lonely your life had become. Instantly, your once dull, predictable, routine days were transformed into a life filled with excitement, romance, joy, laughter, intimacy, companionship ... passion! Then, at the height of this ecstasy, you discover your soul mate is in love with another. In an instant, just as quickly as it began, your love story comes to an abrupt end as once again, you find yourself in the throes of loneliness and depression. Life has cruelly teased you with the sweetness of desire temporarily satisfied.

This bitter reality makes you want to close your eyes to shut out the vision of others experiencing the lasting happiness that eludes you. You want to close your eyes to avoid seeing the inadequacies that seem to be the root cause of your loneliness as, once again; you are forced to deal with the fact that you simply are not good enough. You wonder what is so wrong with you that keeps you from inspiring a lasting love, a lasting respect, a lasting devotion from another. You wonder if you will ever be "good enough" to maintain the affection of that ever-elusive someone special. You wonder if anyone will ever be happy with you just as you are. Deep down you have this sick, nauseating feeling that confirms the answer you dread to accept:

there will always be someone more attractive, more interesting, more sensitive, more creative, funnier, wittier, wealthier ... better. Arriving at this bleak conclusion, you lie there never wanting to open your eyes again so you don't have to see your misery, your shortcomings, or others enjoying the happiness you so desperately desire.

Perhaps you are one of the many affected by economic problems. Maybe you have been left wondering what will become of your financial future. The recent collapse of the housing market and the ensuing credit crisis has touched just about all of us as we have watched a financial tsunami sweep away trillions of dollars in savings and retirement right before our very eyes. You may be one of the millions of people who, after years of hard work, discipline, and sacrifice, have watched your hard-earned capital vanish like the morning mist. For years you exercised discipline in all your investment strategies, you obeyed all the rules, you followed the advice of all the experts, and just when things were looking as if it was about to pay off so you could finally experience that dream retirement, you wake up to the financial nightmare of losing half your nest egg. You are disturbed by thoughts of how much better off you would be had you gotten out of the market right before it began its precipitous fall from those historic highs. Your mind is flooded with the thoughts of all you could have done with the invested money that has now disappeared: the vacations, home improvements, college tuition ... blowing it all in Vegas would have even been better than simply watching it all go up in smoke as the markets went down in flames.

It may be that things have gotten so bad that now you are not only worried about how you're going to make it in retirement, you are also worried about how you're going to make it right now! In this tenuous economic environment, your very job may be in jeopardy. Maybe you too want to close your eyes to escape to a financial dream world where all is well because, quite frankly, reality is too much of a nightmare.

Maybe you are experiencing the humiliation of losing a job, getting laid off, being passed over for a promotion, or desperately, but unsuccessfully, trying to find a new job. These events can be especially demoralizing in light of all the effort, hard work, and dedication you have given to a company or organization in the past. The inestimable sacrifices you have made: the late hours, the missed birthdays, anniversaries, and holidays. For those in the military, putting your very life at risk throughout multiple deployments. After giving everything you have to give and feeling as if you are making a difference, you soon discover that your contributions apparently were really not that significant at all. In fact, your services are no longer necessary. You are expendable. This shakes you to the very core, the very center of your identity, because what you do defines who you are. Right? If your services are no longer necessary that can mean only one thing: you are no longer necessary. You feel as though your very essence is defined by failure. In an instant you have lost your earning power, your status, your sense of worth, your value.

You find yourself withdrawing from society because you don't want to answer the question, "So how's it going?" You withdraw because you don't want to be the object of others' pity. You want others to respect you, not feel sorry for you. Life has knocked you down flat on your back, leaving you looking up to where you used to be. Now you too want nothing more than to just close your eyes to shut out the pain.

Perhaps you have just gone through the heart-wrenching loss of a miscarriage and are tormented by visions of happy couples with newborns, which only

intensify the anguish of your loss. While you would not want to deny those couples their joy, you struggle with the bitterness of your joy being brutally taken away—joy that increased with every visit to the doctor's office, joy that leaped at the first sound of those steady, strong beats of your baby's heart, joy that swelled into pride over the photos the technician took of your little miracle (even though you could not make out heads or tails on that fuzzy screen, you proudly showed those sonogram pictures to all who happened by), joy that thrilled when your baby's first movements could be seen and felt as their little hands and feet pushed against the walls of an increasingly crowded womb.

Like eagerness surrounding a wrapped gift you couldn't wait to open, the anticipation of the joyous birthday built as you tried to imagine what your baby would look like, what color its eyes would be, whose nose it would have, or how much longer you would have to wait until you could feel your infant's hands gently gripping and hugging your finger. Then one day, unexpectedly, amid all those things associated with preparing for your little bundle of joy, amidst all the baby name books, packing for the delivery room trip, all the preparations for the nursery, there is stillness, there is spotting, and there is silence. Your joy is replaced by an overwhelming,

inconsolable sadness. You want nothing more than to close your eyes in the hope that you can soon wake up to find that it was all nothing more than your worst possible dream.

It may be that you are reading this book while grieving over the death of a loved one. No one is ever prepared for the emotional toll associated with the finality of forever losing someone who has been such a vital, integral part of your life—a part of life that had become as important and necessary as the very air to breathe. But now, in death, that air is gone. The mere thought of a single tomorrow without that spouse, child, parent, relative, or friend is unimaginable, so the reality of bereavement for the remainder of your life causes tears and sobs to flow with such violence that your head aches and your legs tingle. Mercilessly, that unimaginable tomorrow becomes reality today as you slowly awaken to an existence completely foreign to you, an existence void of the person you just buried, with no hope of him rejoining you on the journey of life to share its experiences. Yet, your mind is slow to accept this reality as you still sense that he is with you or even find yourself calling his name, fully expecting him to answer. When he does not respond, the weight of sorrow is so great and tangible that you feel it

crushing your very bones. This oppressive grief makes you want to lie down and close your eyes to block out the vision of you languishing along life's long, winding road, forced to finish your journey handicapped by the fresh, empty hole in your heart.

For those in the military, perhaps you got knocked down on a mission no different from the hundreds of other missions you had previously been on. The sun was bright and high in the sky, the heat inescapable. One major difference was notable, however. The normally bustling neighborhood and crowded streets were now unusually clear. Try as you might to forget, you remember every detail of what happened in those next few moments: the nauseating concussion from the blast that knocked you over, causing your ears to ring and bleed, the searing heat, pain that cannot be put into words. Above all, you cannot get the haunting sounds of your screaming battle buddies or the pungent smells of burning metal, rubber, and flesh out of your head. The whole scene plays over and over again in your mind's eye, and each time the memory comes, you ask God how He could allow something like that to happen. You know you would have done anything to protect those you love, and it seems a loving God would do the same. You too would like to close your eyes to shut out the visions, the memories, and the guilt.

I don't have the time, space, or ability to graphically detail the emotional responses to abuse, addiction, assault, wayward children, being victimized, being robbed, or any of the myriad other horrible events that affect us in our fallen world. I can, however, summarize these experiences with one word. Helplessness. Feelings of helplessness that if left unchecked inevitably lead to feelings of hopelessness. A sense of hopelessness is what makes us want to close our eyes to the world, to shut ourselves up in a place where life cannot get to us or hurt us anymore, a place where we will never again experience these great pains or this great despair.

If you have suffered this kind of despair, you know how hard it can be to regain your motivation, to renew your hope. What do you do when you reach this point of utter despair? Where do you turn when the world has turned against you? How do you go on? Where do you find the strength to pick yourself up and continue the fight, especially when it seems you don't have any fight left?

This is where we find the disciples in the New Testament gospels after Jesus' crucifixion. This is where the Bible speaks to those in the situations I have just mentioned. This is where the Bible gives hope to the hopeless and help to the helpless. I invite you to fight every urge to keep your eyes closed, and I urge you to open them one more time to see where the Bible tells you to look for inspiration and motivation to stay in the fight when you have hit the very rock bottom of the sea of life.

The disciples came incredibly close to reaching the shores of their ideal. They came incredibly close to realizing their dream of establishing a new kingdom on earth, a kingdom in which each disciple would rule from one of twelve thrones, and a kingdom where they would each receive riches, honor, and respect. After three years of "straining at the oars" to reach the shores of their dreams, a tidal wave of unforeseen circumstances rose up and swept them away from their hopes and dreams. They experienced this loss because Jesus, the one who had given them their hopes and inspired their dreams, had just been brutally executed by the authorities, and the disciples were certain they and their families would now meet with the same fate.

So they shut themselves up in a room where the world could not get to them or hurt them. And there, they closed their eyes to their dreams. They cowered together seeking safety and comfort in their numbers. Any time they heard the marching of soldiers or caught a glimpse of a Roman centurion, their minds would immediately be haunted by visions of whips, thorns, spikes, and blood, as they recalled every vivid detail of every gruesome moment of Christ's crucifixion. I'm sure that in the midst of these conscious nightmares the disciples would replace visions of Jesus with visions of themselves in these grisly scenes. Certainly these manufactured images caused them to shudder with terror.

Eventually, the soldiers would pass, the visions of horror would fade, and the fear would abate. I imagine the disciples would then give a collective sigh of relief as they struggled to catch their breath. In those moments, it is possible they were so gripped by fear that without realizing it they had forgotten to breathe. This was their life now, if indeed you could call it a life.

Perhaps their greatest torment, though, was the indescribable disappointment of a hope crushed. Until

they met Jesus, I'm almost certain that each of them had resigned himself to his respective lot in life. There is nothing to indicate that these men had any sense of ambition or destiny. As far as we know, they never dreamed that history would ever take note that they even existed. They, with the possible exception of Simon the Zealot, were content with eking out a peaceful existence for themselves and their families, without any plans of acquiring power or prominence. Jesus, however, changed all that. Jesus "rescued" them from the sea of obscurity and promised them places in the kingdom—not just any kingdom, but the kingdom of God.

Their association with Jesus propelled them from anonymity to the center stage of the nation's attention. Their heads became filled with visions of prestige and influence. Thoughts of repelling the Roman occupation and ruling the world from one of twelve thrones now danced in their heads. Their self-aggrandizing imaginations began to run wild as they recalled the splendor and riches of Solomon's kingdom, a kingdom where gold and silver were as plentiful in the land as stones. Surely the words of Jesus—"I tell you, one greater than Solomon is here"—must have added unimaginable fuel to the fire of their newfound dreams of wealth, power, prestige, and national pride. How enthralling it must have been for them to envision rulers of kingdoms and empires coming to Israel to see their riches, to come and hear their wisdom and the wisdom of Jesus, as the rulers of old did during Solomon's reign.

Certainly they too would share in the power and wisdom of Jesus, because even He said, "Truly, truly, I say to you, he who believes in Me, the works that I do, he will do also; and greater works than these he will do…"(John 14:12 NASB) How satisfying it would be, they must have imagined, to receive gifts and tribute from those very same rulers who held the Jewish nation in such contempt and disdain. Certainly the glory and splendor of the mighty Roman Empire would pale in comparison to this "Kingdom of God," and these twelve ordinary men had the opportunity of a hundred lifetimes to position themselves perfectly, getting in on the ground floor of this new kingdom. This opportunity changed them. These once sober-minded men were now drunk with ambition to the point that they would often engage in heated arguments about who among them would be the greatest in the new kingdom. Some went as far as jockeying for positions to the immediate left and right of Jesus' throne.

With the death of Jesus, those arguments over who among them would be the greatest in the kingdom must have seemed utterly absurd. For there can be no kingdom where the King has died. And with the death of their King, all dreams of positions, and thrones, and riches, and glory died as well.

For three years they had strained at the oars over the tempestuous sea of life, striving to reach the shores of the kingdom of God. For three years they had been apart from their families, following Jesus. For three years they had abandoned their lives, some of them leaving lucrative careers for the dream of ruling with Him in this kingdom of God. They gambled everything. All twelve went all in for the kingdom. They rolled the dice, betting everything on Jesus. And for what? For Him to die on the cross just outside of Jerusalem, putting them and their families in jeopardy of the same fate? The thought must have crossed their minds that it would have been much better to have never known Jesus than to have met Him and have Him fill their heads with such false hopes.

What must have been especially frustrating for them was that they were so close to realizing their hopes and dreams. The promise of the throne of David being restored, the return of the long-lost glory of the kingdom to Israel (a glory that would surpass that of Solomon's time), and the lasting honor for them and their families seemed within their grasp. Just a few days earlier, they had walked into Jerusalem to a king's welcome as throngs of people shouted, "Hosanna to the Son of David!" "Blessed is he who comes in the name of the Lord!" (Matthew 21:9). Surely Jesus would seize this opportunity of overwhelming public support to establish His kingdom and begin the revolution. Certainly this was the harvest that would make three years' worth of sowing without reaping finally pay off. But how quickly shouts of "Hosanna!" turned to shouts of "Crucify!" How quickly their dreams turned into nightmares. Now, rather than ruling from twelve thrones, they were cowering together in an upper room, fearing for their very lives. The tide of circumstances had swept them away from the shores of their ideal, and they too were afraid to look up. They had given up; they had quit the fight.

It was at this point of collective despair, while hiding together in an upper room, that Jesus appeared to the disciples. The disciples saw the resurrected Jesus, and everything changed. They saw Jesus as they had

never seen Him before, and their lives were forever transformed. When they had completely given up hope, when they had completely accepted defeat, then they saw the risen Savior. They saw the mighty conqueror who had defeated the greatest of all enemies—death. And their lives were forever changed. Where once they had been filled with grief, fear, despair, disappointment, and sorrow, now their lives were characterized by hope, peace, joy, purpose, and excitement.

They gave up hiding in an upper room in favor of proclaiming the coming of the kingdom of God in the public squares. Where once they were petrified by fear to the point of denying Jesus before a mere handmaiden, now they were emboldened by faith enough to defy the authorities' orders to speak no more of Jesus, boldly proclaiming, "We cannot help speaking about what we have seen and heard" (Acts 4:20). And with that statement, those men, whose world had seemed to come to an end, set about turning their world upside-down. All because they saw Jesus!

I saw Jesus in a new way on February 7, 2004. As with the disciples, this vision came at the lowest point in my life. I was in basic training at Fort Jackson, S.C. A few years earlier, my life had been very different. I had finally arrived at everything I dreamed of and worked so hard to achieve. I had finally stepped onto the shores of my ideal existence. At long last, I had graduated seminary, gotten married, become the father of two beautiful children with one on the way, lived in a fantastic home in Colorado Springs with a picturesque view of Pikes Peak greeting me every morning...and found the job of a lifetime. I was a youth minister in Colorado. Do you know how fun it is to be a youth minister in Colorado? Rafting, skiing, camping, golf, concerts, paintball, go-carts, Bible studies…and a paycheck. I remember thinking, *This is it. This is what I have been dreaming about and working so hard for all these years!*

Within three years, I had lost it all. I lost my marriage, my job, my car, and my dignity... I lost my children. I'll spare you the long, dramatic story and wrap it all up in one word: *divorce.*

Now I was at boot camp being marched single file to the drill hall where those of us who wanted to were about to attend Sunday school. I remember wishing that either the drill sergeant would pick up the pace, or that the drill hall would be much closer to the barracks, because the temperatures were abnormally cold, and

the winter wind was especially blustery that morning. The frozen ground beneath our feet made a crunching sound with each rhythmic step as the icy blades of grass broke like brittle sticks under our weight. Just as we were about to reach the drill hall, the drill sergeant unexpectedly gave the command "halt" followed by an equally terse, "right, face." He then circled our small formation in silence for what seemed like an eternity, as though he were searching for the right words to say or to create a dramatic effect to really drive home the point he was about to make—or both. It worked.

While we were standing there in silence, wondering what the drill sergeant was about to do or say, I couldn't help but notice that in this moment all of creation seemed to be one big irony. The sky above was amazingly beautiful. It was cloudless and clear and as brilliant a blue as any sky I could remember. The sun, still in the early stages of its daily journey, was rising steadily higher in blinding splendor, washing the earth below in its life-giving light. It was the type of sky you would associate with a wondrous spring or summer morning. But that wind.

That bone-chilling February wind soon dispelled all such pleasant notions of spring, reminding me that although the sun was striving mightily to warm the land and bring about new life, for now, old man winter held tyrannous sway, refusing to relinquish his control over the earth or arouse it from its lifeless slumber. Despite the beauty and promise of the spring sky above, the earth beneath remained a dead, frozen canvas painted in the drab color of brown dead grass with hauntingly bare trees, mere skeletons of the life they once possessed, dotting the landscape. Yet over it all, the sun was shining brightly, serving as a glorious reminder that winter's death would soon give way to spring's life.

My philosophical observations were rudely interrupted as my drill sergeant ceased circling and, breaking his lengthy silence shouted, "Privates! You go in there, and you do whatever it is you do, and you feel whatever it is you feel, but when you come back out here, remember, you are Soldiers." And with that, he filed us into the drill hall where we attended Sunday school. The message he sent was all too clear: what we were doing in Sunday school was not "Soldierly."

As soon as the door opened, I could understand his fear of us forgetting our military bearing. For just on the other side of that door was every imaginable form of forbidden boot-camp fruit; doughnuts, cookies, chips,

Doritos, soft drinks. It was as if we stepped through a portal into another world. Where we were once met by the shrill, harsh voices of drill sergeants screaming at us, now we were greeted with the warm smiles and welcome hugs of a lovely couple with bright, inviting faces. The atmosphere of that military drill hall was transformed by the sounds of their three young children running, laughing, and playing, a big-screen TV showing Veggie Tales cartoons, and a sound system filling the air with the pleasant sounds of praise music.

You would think such an oasis of familiarity in the midst of this desert of strangeness would have been a welcome respite. In reality, however, it plunged me deeper into depression. At that moment, it was as if life was cruelly taunting me with all that I so dearly missed, reminding me of everything I had lost and left behind. The joy in the praise music filling the air only accentuated how desperately sad I was feeling. The Veggie Tales cartoons brought with them the bittersweet memories of sitting on the floor with my children, watching those very same episodes, my two older children sitting to my immediate left and right as I tried to keep from spilling my bowl of cereal as the youngest squirmed in my lap. I tried to imagine what my children were doing at that moment. Were they getting ready for church? I wished I could be there to brush their hair.

Watching this family minister together was especially painful. They were living right in front of me the life I was supposed to live. I was supposed to be together with my family, not all alone in this strange military world. I was supposed to be the one co-laboring with my spouse for the kingdom, my children in tow. I was supposed to be the one demonstrating to my children what it was to fulfill the Great Commission, helping them catch a passion for the Lord's work of missions, evangelism, and worship. I saw those kids smiling at the Soldiers, sitting in their laps, hugging them, and saying with their sweet little voices, "Thank you for your service; we are praying for you," and my heart broke. My heart broke because I missed my own children so much. My heart broke because I knew that my opportunity to influence them had been forever diminished. My heart broke because I knew I had been forever robbed of their childhood. What I wouldn't have given to hear their voices saying they would pray for others. What I wouldn't have given to have my life back.

Once my life had been filled with love and warmth and

comfort. Now I felt like an orphan, all alone in a cold and impersonal world. I used to awake every morning to the pitter-patter of little feet running down the hallway, my children's voices saying over and over again, "Daddy, Daddy, Daddy!" as they jumped into the bed to give me a kiss and a hug and a get-up-and-get-me-breakfast tickle. Now the crass shouting and cursing of raging drill sergeants rudely and abruptly awakened me. The bare, steel-framed beds, cinder-block walls, cold tile floors, mass herding to the latrines and showers, the shaving of my head, having my every action controlled including when I could speak, what I could say, and where I could go (not even across the street without a "battle buddy"), being told what to wear, how to wear it, and when to wear everything, right down to the ugly brown uniform underwear I was issued, were all part of a cold, impersonal, institutionalizing, dehumanizing machine that worked only to increase my loneliness.

Perhaps the most demoralizing aspect was that after all the hard work and sacrifice of four years of college, three years of seminary, a marriage, a house, a car, four kids, and a divorce, I was now no further along than the 17- and 18-year-olds sitting around me. I was broke, homeless, and lonely. At 32 years of age, I was starting all over again. The tide of circumstances had swept me away from the shores of the ideal that I had worked so hard to reach, and I was powerless to prevent it. I wanted to close my eyes. But then I would not have had the vision that has since changed my life. While lying at rock bottom, drowning in a pool of self-pity, I saw Jesus in a way I had never seen Him before. In that drill hall, in the middle of the Sunday school lesson, while ruminating in self-pity, I lifted my eyes toward heaven in a silent prayer, asking God how this could all be happening to me. While lifting my eyes toward heaven, God brought to my attention the "Soldier's Creed" posted on the wall close to the ceiling. It was a statement we had quoted a hundred times throughout that past week, but for some reason, for the very first time, I saw Jesus in that creedal statement, a creedal statement unlike any written by a church council or denominational convention, but a creedal statement just as accurate and true.

The Soldier's Creed begins with the "Warrior Ethos," which simply says, “I will always place the mission first. I will never accept defeat. I will never quit. I will never leave a fallen comrade.” In that moment, in that drill hall, the Holy Spirit spoke to my heart revealing that if the essence of a warrior is defined in that ethos, then

Jesus is the Greatest Warrior, because Jesus always places the mission first, Jesus never quits, Jesus never accepts defeat, and Jesus never leaves a fallen comrade. With that realization, my life was forever changed. It was as if God spoke to me saying, “I have not forgotten My mission of completing the good work I began in you. I will always place that mission first. I will never accept defeat for you. I will never quit you, and I will never leave you in your fallen condition.”

Listen, my friend, no matter how badly you want to close your eyes to shut out the pain and disappointment of this life, I ask you to keep them open. Keep them open for the next few chapters to see, through the eyes of faith, how Jesus lived the Warrior Ethos on your behalf and what that means for you when the tide of circumstances sweeps you away from the ideal to the point that you feel all hope is lost. We will look at how Jesus' living out of the Warrior Ethos means you can rest in the heat of the battle for your life, knowing that just as the Lord went before the children of Israel to fight their battles, Jesus, the Greatest Warrior, will fight for you, living the Warrior Ethos on your behalf.

We will look at how this new vision of Jesus can transform your life, as Jesus' appearance forever changed the disciples' lives from one of hopelessness, helplessness, loneliness, and despair, to lives of hope, strength, joy, and purpose. When you realize that Jesus always places the mission of your blessing first, that Jesus will never accept defeat for you, that Jesus will never quit you and that He will never leave you in your fallen condition, your life will forever be transformed. Let's look first at how our lives can be transformed by knowing Jesus always places the mission first.

Chapter 1: Jesus Always Places the Mission First

There have been times when I wondered if God knew about or cared about my situation. There have been times in my life when I wondered why my prayers were seemingly going unanswered. There have been times in my life when I wondered why God's promises in the Bible were not ringing true in my experience. During those times I was tempted to cry out, "God, are You there? Do you see what is happening to me? Do you care? I'm dying down here!" I wanted to say those things because I felt that God had forgotten about me and didn't understand how much pain I was in or how lonely I felt. If God loved me He would answer my prayers and either (a) never let me go through this or

(b) deliver me from it immediately. I was so consumed with my self-absorbed perspective that I didn't consider that not only did God know and understand what I was going through, He had also already experienced everything I was enduring Himself, but to a much greater degree.

Not until I saw that first line of the Warrior Ethos—"I will always place the mission first"—and God brought to my mind the vision of Jesus praying in the Garden of Gethsemane—"Yet not My will, but Yours be done" (Luke 22:42 NASB)—did I realize that God knew just what I was going through. Not only did He know what I was going through, He also experienced what I was going through in the very mission that led to my salvation. This immediately changed my demeanor for two reasons: (1) because God knew experientially what I was going through, He was sensitive and compassionate toward my situation and (2) because He had, to a much greater degree, experienced the pain and suffering I was experiencing in placing His mission of my salvation first in the past, I could be confident that He would successfully place the mission of my salvation first in the present and continue to successfully place the mission of my salvation first in the future! That is when God finally got my eyes off

myself and on to Christ to see what it cost Jesus to place the mission of my salvation first.

Have you ever thought about what it cost Jesus to place the mission of our salvation first? My own suffering gave me a deeper understanding and a greater appreciation for the price Jesus paid to "deploy" to earth for 33 years on His mission of securing my salvation. Through the prism of my own experiences I caught, as Moses did in the cleft of the rock, just a glimpse of the glory of the great sacrifice Jesus made in putting His mission of salvation first. Through my suffering, I began to realize that Jesus experienced everything I experienced but to a much greater degree.

As I compared my fall from the shores of the ideal to Christ's voluntary fall from glory to earth, I realized my experience couldn't begin to compare to what He went through. This gave me a fresh understanding of how much He loves me. For in spite of the great sacrifice involved in the mission of securing our salvation, He still placed that mission first, proving His overwhelming love for me. Let me provide a few examples to explain.

When saddened by memories of waking every morning to the precious sounds of my children saying, "Daddy,

Daddy, Daddy" over and over again to the new reality of rude awakenings by raging, cursing drill sergeants shouting harshly, I would consider the great loneliness Jesus must have experienced. He went from being constantly heralded by the perfect praise of adoring angels singing in glory, "Holy, holy, holy is the Lord God Almighty" (Revelation 4:8), to his new reality of the cruel and undeserved shouts of an angry mob shouting, "Crucify Him, crucify Him, crucify Him!" (Matthew 27:22).

While crawling out of my cold, damp sleeping bag or reluctantly pulling myself out of that old, uncomfortable bottom bunk in the barracks, I would often reminisce about the plush surroundings of my former life compared to the drab, steel-frame beds, unadorned cinder-block walls, and cold, hard tile floors of my new austere, Spartan surroundings. I would then think about how much greater a contrast Jesus experienced foregoing the opulence of heaven for the primitive surroundings of a manger. What a contrast the dirt roads, humble abodes, and cold, wet nights of earth must have been to the golden streets, bejeweled mansions, and temperate climate Jesus enjoyed in glory. In light of that contrast, the statement that "foxes have holes and birds of the air have nests, but the Son of Man has no place to lay his head" (Matthew 8:20) takes on a whole new level of profoundness. Imagine the Creator, sustainer, and owner of all creation having nowhere to lay His head.

While shivering in the cold with no prospect of warmth; while sleeping on the ground, exposed to the elements with no sanctuary from the wind and rain; while trudging through the muck, the mud, and the sand with no solid ground to put my feet upon; while wallowing in sweat from the sweltering, unrelenting heat, with no opportunity to shed any of the heavy gear covering me from head to toe, I would often wish for just a moment to escape every misery, to relieve every discomfort, to surrender to every base inclination for the creature comforts of home. During those times, my most noble ambition would be for nothing more than a shower, a brief moment in the shade, a cool breeze, to be dry, to be warm, to be comfortable, to sleep, to enjoy the life I once knew. Going so abruptly from a life filled with the comforts and amenities of modern society to the harsh, rugged life of military training and deployments was a shock to my system. During those times I would often think about the shock it must have been for Jesus to go from perfection in heaven to imperfection here on earth. How He must have been haunted by memories of the comfort and ease He enjoyed in eternity.

There is no deprivation any human can experience to match the level of contrast experienced by Christ in putting His mission first. We can never know what it is to go from perfection to want. Try to imagine the one who is the self-replenishing source of life and energy, the one who upholds all things by the power of His word, the one who never sleeps nor slumbers, being, in His humanity, exhausted to the point of sleeping through a storm in the stern of a boat. Omnipotence sleeping in humanity is a contrast we can never experience, a mystery we can never comprehend.

...the Father who once said, "This is my Son, whom I love; with him I am well pleased" (Matthew 3:17), would soon be "pleased" to bruise Him on the cross.

Try to imagine the one who is the bread of life being hungry and in need of bread. Try to imagine the one who is the source of life-giving water, the one from whom streams of living water flow, the one who promises to satisfy the thirst of all who would come to

Him for drink, hanging on a cross and crying out, "I thirst" (John 19:28 KJV). This is a contrast you and I could never begin to understand.

Yet Jesus understood perfectly that whatever privation He experienced in His life was but a small taste of what He would experience in His death. He understood all too well that the most satisfying, sacred, and divine fellowship to be experienced—the fellowship He enjoyed with His Father from eternity past—would soon be severed. He understood that the Father who once said, "This is my Son, whom I love; with him I am well pleased" (Matthew 3:17), would soon be "pleased" to bruise Him on the cross. That understanding horrified Him.

The thought of being bruised and crushed to the point of death for our iniquities horrified Him. For in death, Jesus would experience what, for Him, was unimaginable—separation from God. The thought of being separated from that most blessed fellowship is what pressed the lifeblood from His pores, forcing the words from His mouth: "My Father, if it is possible, may this cup be taken from me" (Matthew 26:39). The words Jesus uttered after that prayer constitute the most significant sentence ever uttered from human lips: "Yet not as I will, but as you will" (Matthew 26:39).

Jesus prayed, "Not as I will," because Jesus always places the mission first. He chose mission first even when that mission involved the ridicule of man, the discomfort and poverty of earth, the shame and pain of the cross, the death of hell, and the incalculable sacrifice of separation from the Father. In spite of the suffering, in spite of the sacrifice, in spite of the separation, Jesus yielded and said, "Nevertheless, not my will, but Yours be done," because Jesus always places the mission first!

We live in a world of disclaimers. Disclaimers like "Results not typical," or "Past performance is no guarantee of future results." With Jesus, past performance *is* a guarantee of future results. Your future is secure because of what Jesus performed in the past. The same Jesus who placed the mission of your salvation first in the Garden of Gethsemane is the very same Jesus who now places the mission of *you* first. You are now His mission:

> I am confident of this very thing, that He who began a good work in you will perfect it until the day of Christ Jesus. (Philippians 1:6)

Regardless of how dire your present circumstances may be, because of Jesus, you are destined for glory. Romans 8:29-30 states:

> For those God knew he also predestined to be conformed to the likeness of his Son, that he might be the firstborn among many brothers. And those he predestined, he also called; those he called, he also justified; those he justified, he also glorified.

According to Romans 8:29, regardless of how dismal your present circumstances may be or how much pain you are enduring, because of Jesus, you are destined for glory. And as I heard over and over again in boot camp, "Pain is temporary, but glory is forever!"

Pain causes many people to lose their faith. I guess it is all how you look at things. For me, the pain increased my faith. When I realized that the pain of rejection, loss, separation, suffering, and deprivation I experienced was but a small taste of what Jesus experienced in this world to redeem me, I gained a deeper appreciation for what it cost Him to place the mission of my redemption first. The pain I experienced was but a small taste of what Jesus experienced in this world, because as God is greater than us to an infinite degree, so the pain He endured was greater than ours to an infinite degree. As I pondered that thought, I gained a better understanding of how much He was willing to go through to restore me.

When I was reeling from the pain of rejection from my divorce, I understood a little better how God must have felt at the Garden of Eden, and every day since, as humanity continues to reject Him. He says as much when He tells the prophet in Ezekiel 6:9,

> "Those who escape will remember me—how I have been grieved by their adulterous hearts, which have turned away from me, and by their eyes, which have lusted after their idols."

When I feel like those closest to me have abandoned me and turned their backs on me, leaving me all alone, I catch just a glimpse of what Jesus must have felt when the disciples deserted Him and His Father forsook Him. When I have given in my relationships

until it hurts, only to have my sacrifices be taken for granted, unappreciated, and unrecognized, I understand a little better how God must feel when I fail to thank Him for all He has done in my life and instead complain about Him not doing more on my behalf.

When I work hard and sacrifice and save trying to get one step ahead financially, only to have circumstances knock me two steps back, I understand a little better how frustrated God must get when He has given so much and worked so hard to bring about a harvest of righteousness in me, only to reap the bitter fruit of sin, selfishness, and pride from the field of my life.

Whenever my kids are too busy to talk to me or have other things they would rather do or other people they would rather see than spend time with me, I understand a little better how much the Father's great heart must break when I am too busy to spend time with Him or would rather do other things than give myself to His life and work.

When I remember how hard it was to see my son in the hospital, or how much it hurt my heart to lose my third child in miscarriage, or when I shudder at the thought of this world hurting my children in any way, I catch just

a glimpse of how painful it must have been for the eternal Father to watch His Son be rejected, ridiculed, abused, and killed.

Yet despite all the pain and suffering I cause Him, God still loves me, God still sacrifices, and God still places the mission of my salvation first. The pain taught me about God's love in a way that His blessings never did. It made me more certain than ever of God's presence and victory in my life. The pain taught me how much it cost Jesus to place the mission of my salvation first... our salvation first. I was forever changed.

Realizing what it cost Jesus to place the mission first changed the questions I was asking. I no longer asked, "How could God allow these horrible things to happen to me so unfairly?" but rather, "How could God allow these horrible things to happen to Jesus so unfairly, to spare me from all the things I so fairly deserve?"

Realizing what it cost Jesus to place the mission first changed the bitterness I was feeling. How could I remain bitter knowing my fall couldn't begin to compare to Christ's descent from the heights of heaven to the depths of the grave, a descent on my behalf, for my benefit? How could I remain bitter toward God,

knowing my fall was justly deserved, owing, in part, to my mistakes and sins, while Christ's fall was unjustly deserved, owing completely to my mistakes and my sins?

Realizing what it cost Jesus to place the mission first changed the beliefs I was holding. How could I continue in despair, believing my situation would never improve, knowing that, to the praise and glory of His grace, Jesus always places the mission of my salvation first? How could I believe that, having paid such a high price to secure my salvation, Jesus would now abandon the mission He began in me? How can you, beloved, after Jesus has so faithfully demonstrated His willingness to always place the mission of your salvation first, continue in despair, believing your situation will never improve?

Do not lose faith in the midst of your pain. Do not lose faith in God. Do not lose faith because you have the mistaken idea that a good God would never allow you to suffer. That would be true if Adam and Eve had never sinned originally. A good God would never allow anyone to suffer in the world of the Garden of Eden, but Adam and Eve's disobedience removed us from that world. Now we live in this world, and Jesus says,

"In this world, you will have trouble" (John 16:33). This is a world filled with disappointment, discomfort, debt, depressions, deployments, defilement, disaster, depression, divorce, disease, and death. But Jesus goes on to say, "Take heart! I have overcome the world" (John 16:33). This is a great comfort indeed, because it reveals that Jesus is intimately acquainted with our suffering. Overcoming this world required Jesus engaging this world. Rest assured, whatever pain, whatever disappointment, whatever sadness, whatever bad experience you are going through or have ever gone through, Jesus experienced it, endured it, and overcame it. This is why the Bible says:

> "We do not have a high priest who cannot sympathize with our weaknesses, but one who has been tempted in all things as we are, yet without sin. Therefore let us draw near with confidence to the throne of grace, so that we may receive mercy and find grace to help in time of need." (Hebrews 4:15-16)

In Isaiah 49:15–16 we have this promise from God:

> "Can a mother forget the baby at her breast and have no compassion on the child she has

> borne? Though she may forget, I will not forget you! See, I have engraved you on the palms of my hands; your walls are ever before me."

Because Jesus overcame the world, on the promise of God's infallible Word, you have every confidence of finding help in your time of need. With Jesus, that result is typical!

You can think, "If God loved me, I wouldn't be going through this," or you can think, "God would not have gone through this if He didn't love me."

In your time of need, you are always confronted with a choice. You can choose to see your pain as proof that God doesn't love you and abandon your faith, or you can see your pain as proof that God does love you because your pain is but a small taste of what Jesus experienced to redeem you. Such a perspective will result in your faith being strengthened. You can think, "If God loved me, I wouldn't be going through this," or you can think, "God would not have gone through this if He didn't love me."

Take heart! In your time of disappointment, discomfort, debt, defilement, disaster, depression, deployment, divorce, disease, and even death, you have a deliverer! Because you have a deliverer who overcame the world in the past, you can know that you have a deliverer who overcomes the world in the present. You have a deliverer who feels your pain. You have a deliverer who is on mission for your benefit. You have a deliverer who is faithful to complete the mission He began in you, and you have a deliverer who always places that mission first. Take heart! For you have a deliverer who, in that mission, never accepts defeat!

Chapter 2: Jesus Never Accepts Defeat

There were times during Jesus' ministry when it seemed that all had been lost. One of those times was the death of Lazarus. On the occasion of Lazarus' illness, his sisters did exactly what they should have done. They immediately sent word to Jesus, saying, "Lord, the one You love is sick" (John 11:3). In the past, Jesus had often gone out of his way to heal a complete stranger, prompted by nothing more than a simple request. Certainly Jesus would respond to the request of a friend on behalf of someone Jesus knew and loved. When Jesus received news that Lazarus was seriously ill, He lingered for two days before leaving for Bethany. He didn't linger because He didn't love Lazarus and Martha and Mary; He lingered because

He loved Lazarus and Martha and Mary. Read the following verses in John 11:5-6 paying close attention to the words now and so:

“Now Jesus loved Martha and her sister and Lazarus. So when He heard that he was sick, He then stayed two days longer in the place where He was."

When Jesus finally arrived, Lazarus had been dead for four days. Why would Jesus delay coming to the aid of His deathly ill friend? Why, if He loved Lazarus and Mary and Martha, would He not come right away? Some might say that if Jesus really loved Lazarus, He would have dropped everything and run immediately to Bethany to heal His friend, preventing him from any further suffering or death. Why would Jesus not do what He did for the centurion’s servant and simply speak a word of healing from where He was, healing Lazarus instantly over great distance? But healing Lazarus, saving him from death, was not what Jesus had in mind. In fact, He told His disciples:

> "This sickness will not end in death. No, it is for God’s glory so that God’s Son may be glorified through it... Lazarus is dead, and for your sake I

> am glad I was not there, so that you may believe." (John 11:14-15)

He then said to Martha,

> “I am the resurrection and the life. He who believes in me will live, even though he dies; and whoever lives and believes in me will never die. Do you believe this?” (John 11:25-26)

Jesus reveals His motivation in allowing the death of Lazarus most clearly in the prayer He prays right before this most spectacular miracle:

> "But I said this for the benefit of the people standing here, that they may believe that you sent me." (John 11:42)

Lazarus’ death and his resurrection through Jesus would give the people a new and compelling reason to believe that God sent Jesus. That is why delaying His arrival to Bethany and allowing Lazarus to die was the most loving thing Jesus could have done. Jesus had already demonstrated that He had power to heal disease in this life. Had he swooped into Bethany just in time to heal Lazarus before he died, Jesus would not have shown them anything new or revealed anything greater about Himself than He had already demonstrated in His previous miracles. By delaying His arrival and allowing Lazarus to die, Jesus demonstrated something greater than the power to heal in this life—He would demonstrate the power of resurrection in the life to come. He would demonstrate the power of life everlasting. Allowing Lazarus to die gave his followers a new reason to believe that in Jesus—even if they died—they would live forever. This is the greatest miracle He could have given them. This is the greatest gift He could have bestowed upon them. Raising Lazarus from the dead was a far more loving act than healing him, as they had asked Him to do.

Although Jesus had His reasons for allowing Lazarus' death, no one else knew or understood those reasons. To all others, Lazarus' situation seemed hopeless. Lazarus had died. Everyone accepted death. Everyone accepted defeat. The disciples didn't even want Jesus to go to Judea, because they were afraid of the Jews who wanted to stone Him. When Jesus insisted that they go anyway, Thomas sarcastically stated, "Let us also go, that we may die with Him" (John 11:16). Thomas and the disciples not only accepted defeat;

they expected it. But Jesus neither expects nor accepts defeat, ever.

Many of the Jews observing from the sidelines began to grumble among themselves saying, "Could not he who opened the eyes of the blind man have kept this man from dying?" Could there not be found a subtle accusation in their question? Could they not be accusing Jesus of avoiding a confrontation with an illness that He could not heal? Was the real reason Jesus delayed in coming because this was an illness too great for Him to handle? Could the delay be a stall tactic to avoid a public failure? They questioned Jesus because they accepted defeat.

Martha accepted defeat when she accused Jesus of missing His window of opportunity by telling Him, "Lord, if You had been here, my brother would not have died" (John 11:22). Case closed.

I am fascinated by how Jesus handled her comment. Jesus knew what He was up to and what He planned to accomplish in this situation, but Martha and Mary had no idea why Jesus had delayed in coming. All they knew was that their brother Lazarus was dead, and if Jesus had been there, Lazarus would still be alive. I am fascinated by the fact that Jesus didn't clue Martha in. He didn't say to her, "Now just calm down Martha…I let Lazarus die on purpose so that other people could see that I have the power of life and death and that I am the resurrection and the life. I let your brother die because I love you in a special way and therefore want to do a special miracle that will bring special glory to me." Jesus did not give Martha an explanation; He simply gave her truth.

> "Your brother will rise again." (John 11:23)

> "I am the resurrection and the life; he who believes in Me will live even if he dies, and everyone who lives and believes in Me will never die. Do you believe this?" (John 11:25-26)

I believe the message that God wants to communicate to us is this: when we can't see His hand in our situation, when we don't understand why He doesn't answer our prayers the way we think He should if He really loved us, when we don't know why He has allowed horrible things to happen to us, we should hold fast to the truth we do know. Jesus is the resurrection and the life, and everything that He does or allows is motivated by His love and will ultimately lead to His

glory and our good. Even if we die. What God wants to communicate to us in this passage is: when circumstances hide the purposes of God, God bids us to cling to what we do know. We know that God is love, God is true, God is holy, God is just, and God is good. God, then, apart from explanation, in the midst of our circumstances asks each and every one of us that most important question:

> "Do you believe this?" (John 11:25)

To Martha's credit, she did follow up that statement with the assertion, "But I know that even now God will give you whatever you ask" (John 11:22). "Yes, Lord," she told Him, "I believe that you are the Christ, the Son of God, who was to come into the world" (John 11:27). But even then she did not really believe that Jesus could affect her current situation. When Jesus told her that her brother would rise again, she said, "I know he will rise again in the resurrection at the last day" (John 11:24). Sure, she believed Jesus was the Son of God, able to secure victory for all of eternity at some point in the distant future, on the last day; but for now, for the present, she had accepted defeat. Why else, when Jesus ordered the stone rolled back, would she have stated the obvious: "By this time there is a bad odor, for

he has been there four days"? (John 11:39). She objected to what was required for life anew because in her lack of faith, in death, she had accepted defeat. Jesus never accepts defeat.

Mary also accepted defeat: "When Martha heard that Jesus was coming, she went out to meet him, but Mary stayed at home" (John 11:20). This same Mary, whom Jesus at one time had praised for setting aside all other concerns in favor of sitting at His feet, now couldn't even rouse herself to greet Jesus upon hearing of His arrival. Jesus had to call for her. Where was the love and devotion that Mary once showed for Jesus when she abandoned all sense of decorum, lavishly displaying her devotion to Jesus by anointing His feet with a costly perfume worth a year's wages, then wiping those same perfumed feet with her hair? What happened to the Mary who wanted nothing more than to sit at those very same anointed feet drinking up every word pouring from the divine lips of Jesus? What happened to the Mary who once took such delight in simply being in the presence of Jesus? She was gone. She abandoned her desire to be with Jesus because, as far as she was concerned, Jesus had abandoned her at the point of her greatest need. When she and

her brother needed Jesus most, Jesus was not there, and now, Lazarus had died.

Mary felt betrayed. Mary accepted defeat. She too said to Jesus, "Lord, if You had been here, my brother would not have died" (John 11:32). Can you hear the accusation in her voice? Can you sense the hurt? Can you feel the double pain of the bereavement of a brother and the betrayal of a friend? "Lord, if You had been here! Why couldn't You have been here? What was so important that You couldn't come when we called? We have seen You leave straightway and travel great distances to heal the loved ones of complete strangers because You had compassion for them. You didn't even have to bother Yourself to leave on our account, Jesus. You could have simply spoken the words of healing to Lazarus, and those healing words would have traveled to their appointed destination, instantly bringing Your miraculous touch over great distances as You did for the centurion. You didn't even know the centurion! But for us? When we, Your friends, need You, You are so busy meeting the needs of others in some remote part of the region that you can't even take a brief moment of time to speak a simple word? Jesus, You stayed at our house! We gave You food, and shelter, and clothing, and supported You in Your ministry. We honored You and welcomed You as part of the family. We have never asked You for anything. Lord, if You had been here, my brother would not have died!"

The Bible does not record Mary communicating all these doubts and accusations in words, but it may have been what the Bible meant when it says, "Martha... went out to meet Him, but Mary stayed at home" (John 11:20). Sometimes we say more by our actions than we ever do with our words. Her staying at home indicated that she had accepted defeat.

Jesus had never done anything to cause such doubt or disbelief. I'm sure there were many reasons for the intense emotion recorded in that most concise verse, "Jesus wept" (John 11:35). Perhaps the pervasive sense of defeat in the hearts of those to whom Jesus had been so faithful or the persistent disbelief they seemed to cling to were the sources of His great sadness that day. It must still sadden the heart of the Almighty when we doubt His ability, when we question His love, when we second-guess the wisdom of His timing. It must hurt Him when, after He has time and again demonstrated nothing but faithfulness, love, and wisdom, we still weep and mourn because we refuse to believe that He is able to cause all things to work together for the good of those who love Him. Choosing instead to accept the apparent defeat that is, rather than rejoicing in anticipation of the victory that is to come. It must hurt Him when we stay at home. We must never trust in our own assessment of the situation, no matter how dire that situation might be. We must never surrender to defeat, no matter how conclusive the evidence is to the contrary. Remember, when all hope seems lost, Jesus never accepts defeat.

This was never more apparent than on the occasion of Christ's own death. For years Jesus had been preaching the coming of the kingdom of God. His words of hope and change inspired the hearts of all those who followed Him and were the source of their devotion to Him. They believed that Jesus was going to establish a kingdom where justice, equality, peace, and prosperity would be available to everyone. They believed the yoke of oppression they had worn for generations was going to be eternally and victoriously thrown off with the dawning of a new day—a day when Israel would emerge from the fetters of Roman rule as a sovereign, independent nation—a day when the world would recognize the superiority of this everlasting kingdom of God, whose throne would be firmly established and centered in Jerusalem. Just when this dream was about to be realized, just as Jesus was at the height of His popularity, things took a dramatic turn for the worse. Like an untimely darkness, the glory of the hope of Jesus and His promised kingdom seemed to be eclipsed by the Jewish authorities, the Roman rulers, and the multitudes, which with one voice called for His crucifixion. As the great heart of Jesus broke on the cross, pouring out a mixture of blood and water, the pulse of hope stopped within the hearts of the disciples. As the heart of Christ stopped, so stopped the heart of the movement. Everyone accepted defeat for Jesus and the movement that would become known as Christianity.

The enemies of Jesus believed they had defeated Him. They immediately went to Pilate to ask that a unit of Roman soldiers be detached to the burial site of Jesus, not because they believed they needed to keep Jesus in the grave but because they were afraid that the disciples would come and steal the body.

> "So give the order for the tomb to be made secure until the third day. Otherwise, his disciples may come and steal the body and tell the people that he has been raised from the

> dead. This last deception will be worse than the first." (Matthew 27:64)

The Pharisees and Sadducees weren't concerned about Jesus rising from the dead; they believed they had defeated Him. They were worried about His disciples stealing the body. They overestimated His disciples and underestimated Him.

They need not have worried about the disciples; the disciples were not brave enough to steal the body. The disciples were far too scared and defeated themselves to carry out such a daring mission. They were scattered and hiding like whimpering pups, trembling for their very lives in the upper room. The disciples were eminently concerned that they would meet the same fate as Jesus. There was no hopeful anticipation among the disciples at the memory of Jesus' words that He would be crucified, buried, and raised again three days later. They didn't believe His words. They didn't believe His words, because they believed that at Calvary, Jesus had been defeated.

The women, who had shown the most courage by being at the foot of the cross to the bitter end, didn't believe Jesus either. Though they demonstrated a loyalty to Jesus that surpassed that of the disciples by lovingly attending to His body at the grave, they didn't believe Jesus would be victorious. They did not go to the tomb that morning looking for a living, conquering Savior; they did not go to the grave with great joy in anticipation of greeting the risen Lord. They went to the grave to anoint the body of a dead man. The only thing they believed was that Jesus had been defeated. They did not weep tears of great joy when they found the tomb empty; they wept tears of great sorrow, because they thought someone had moved His body. Instead of rejoicing, they cried and begged the angel of the Lord, whom they mistook for a common gardener, to tell them where the body of their dead leader had been taken. They begged and cried for the missing body of Jesus, because they believed Jesus had been defeated.

The demons and the evil one surely also believed that Jesus was defeated. How else could they have interpreted the shrill cry of Jesus asking, "My God, My God, why have You forsaken me?" (Matthew 27:46). How their sick, twisted joy must have welled up within them when, at the height of midday, the earth turned completely dark as God turned His back on His only begotten Son. What else could that mean but the defeat of Jesus?

Everyone believed that Jesus had been defeated: Pilate, Herod, Caiaphas, the Pharisees, the Sadducees, the disciples, the women, the crowds, the demons… everyone. When faced with the choice of believing the words of Jesus promising resurrection or trusting their own senses and rational thought, they chose human reason over divine promises. They trusted the evidence. Rather than believe the sure testimony of Jesus, they believed the beatings, the hemorrhaging, the thorns, the nails, the last breath, the spear, and the ensuing geyser of blood and water that poured forth from the side of Jesus. They believed the order to take His lifeless body off the cross. They believed the burial preparations. They believed the entombment of Christ's lifeless body. Everyone, without exception, believed that this seemingly overwhelming amount of evidence pointed to but one conclusion: Jesus had been defeated.

They didn't consider God's faithfulness to Israel as recorded in Scripture or the countless prophecies fulfilled therein. They didn't call to mind the life of Jesus and the many miraculous works He had performed before their very eyes. They didn't remember that His word had calmed the seas, restored sight to the blind, healed withered hands, caused the lame to walk, and exercised dominion over evil spirits. They didn't consider that the one who had walked on water, predicted future events, and raised the dead to life could also make good on His promise to come back from the grave. They didn't meditate on the Old Testament Scripture that said:

> "You know with all your heart and soul that not one of all the good promises the Lord your God gave you has failed. Every promise has been fulfilled; not one has failed." (Joshua 23:14)

Rather than believe the unfailing Word of God, they trusted the imperfect understanding of human rationale. Rather than rejoicing at what was to come, they mourned over what had happened. Those followers of Christ are not to be criticized for grieving the cruel, unjust execution of Jesus; they are to be criticized for mourning as those who had no hope. They are to be criticized because they mourned the crucifixion on Friday as if the resurrection on Sunday was never going to happen. They are to be criticized for being faithless. But praise God that when we are faithless, He remains faithful. While the demons rejoiced in defiance, the Romans washed their hands in guilt, the Jews secured the tomb in precaution, the disciples hid in fear, and the women mourned in defeat, Jesus arose in triumph—because Jesus never accepts defeat.

Do not make the same mistake His followers made after the crucifixion. Do not believe your circumstances more than you believe God's sovereignty. Do not believe your problem more than you believe God's promises. Do not believe your worry more than you believe God's Word. Do not accept defeat, but through faith, accept victory in Jesus—because Jesus never accepts defeat.

There are times when my struggles, failures, shortcomings, and personal defeat do cause me to question whether or not I have exceeded the patience of God. I often wonder if God has given up on me the way I have given up on myself so many times. That is when I remind myself that Jesus, the Greatest Warrior who never accepts defeat, is also Jesus, the Greatest Warrior, who never quits.

Chapter 3:
Jesus Never Quits

Many people begin a tough assignment only to grow "weary in well doing,"(Galatians 6:9) aborting the mission when it becomes too difficult, substituting mission first with their own comfort, convenience, personal rights and agenda first.

As I sat in the drill hall that morning during Sunday school, contemplating how Jesus demonstrated and fulfilled the Warrior Ethos as the Greatest Warrior to ever live, I couldn't help but think of all the times and all the things I had quit in my past. The exercise programs I quit because the results did not come quickly enough. The music lessons that I never saw through to mastery because I was not willing to put in the time or effort. The many New Year's resolutions I gave up on because I did not have the willpower or fortitude to keep them. The jobs I quit because the situation got too difficult or because I didn't see any hope of things ever improving. The relationships I quit because I was not being treated as I felt I deserved to be treated, giving up on people and hurting those I cared about most.

These reflections forced me to see that I had something to do with the pain and suffering I was enduring. The decisions I had made in the past were part of the reason why I was where I was in the present. This forced me to take some of the responsibility for my situation. Being reminded of my personal failures not only forced me to take personal responsibility for my situation, but also served as a contrast to magnify Jesus' many successes. He never quit.

Since that Sunday morning, there have been many times when I have compared my situation to that of Jesus' experience. There were times during physical fitness tests when I wanted to quit because my lungs were burning and my sides were aching with a pain that felt as if someone was trying to pull my ribs out. There were times during those long marches, carrying 50 to 60 pounds of gear, when all I wanted was to quit and lie down on the side of the road, because the load on my back seemed too great to bear and the blisters on my feet were too painful for me to continue. There were days when I didn't think I could take any more yelling or "corrective training." I just wanted to walk away.

Some nights during our deployment in Iraq, the loneliness was so intense that I wanted desperately to quit and run back to the life I once knew, seeking the comfort of friends and family back home. During those times, I was always encouraged when I compared my experience to that of Jesus' while He was here on earth. He didn't quit the disciples when they were slow to learn or didn't want to learn. He didn't quit the disciples when they deserted, denied, and cursed Him. He didn't quit the crowds when they continually pressed Him for more teaching, more feeding, and more healing, even though He knew those very same crowds would soon turn on Him, calling for His crucifixion. Most amazingly, He didn't quit the will of God when He was tempted in mind, body, and spirit to deviate from the commands of God.

Thirty-three years of sinless perfection. Each time I resolve to not repeat a thought, an action, a speech pattern, a sin…and fail, I am reminded of the wonder of the sinlessness of Christ. After each failure of mine, I think of the words of the apostle Paul, who said, "I do not understand what I do. For what I want to do I do not do, but what I hate I do… What a wretched man I am! Who will rescue me from this body of death?" (Romans 7:15, 24).

I can identify with that. I am both frustrated and confused by the fact that I am, at times, powerless to carry through with what I am so determined to accomplish, while at other times, I am so powerless to prevent the actions I am absolutely determined to quit. Although Jesus had these temptations, He did not have this struggle. He was able to say, "I always do what pleases him [God]" (John 8:29). I grow more and more amazed each day at Jesus' ability, in His humanity, to subject His flesh to the will of the Father. Sinless perfection! He alone is worthy to be praised. Equally impressive is His ability to exercise His will in enduring the intense suffering of the cross.

Jesus was never subjected to forces outside of His ability to control. By way of illustration, imagine someone being asked to sacrifice his life for another's by being burned at the stake. If that person agrees to sacrifice himself to spare another, he would surrender first to the force of the executioners tying him to the stake before the fire is started, then to the force of the ropes keeping him tied to the stake once those fires have been lit. Try as he might to escape, he would be forced to endure because of the ropes constraining him.

Now imagine the degree of love and the strength of will of one who gives his life for another by enduring to the death the fires of sacrifice, apart from the external constraints of any ropes to bind him. Imagine someone motivated simply by love for another walking willingly into the flames and, constrained by nothing more than the sheer power of his will, clinging voluntarily to the wooden stake while the flames engulf him to his very last breath.

That is the best analogy I can think of to explain what occurred on Calvary. Jesus was never subjected to forces outside of His control. Jesus took great pains to explain that no man took His life, but that He Himself

laid it down freely. Jesus told Pilate that Pilate had no power except that which was given to him. Jesus told the Sanhedrin that He had the power to lay His life down and to take it up again. Jesus told Peter to put away his sword because He had the power of 10,000 angels at His disposal, ready to do His bidding the instant He commanded.

The clearest example of Jesus' life being given and not taken is recorded in the book of Mark, when the authorities and about a hundred soldiers came looking for Jesus in the Garden of Gethsemane to arrest Him. When the authorities asked Him if He was Jesus of Nazareth, Jesus simply said, "I am" (John 18: 6). When Jesus said, "I am," all those assembled to take Him by force fell to the ground, knocked down by nothing other than the sheer power of His word. The power of the voice that spoke all of creation into existence was muted that evening to prevent the complete annihilation of those authorities, but the force of His voice was not muted to the point that no one present that evening did not know they were in the presence of someone with much more power than they could control. Make no mistake—no one took the life of Jesus. He gave it freely. He gave it apart from the constraints of any outside force compelling Him to endure His suffering. At any point, Jesus could have said, "I've had enough!" and freed Himself from the torture and agony of the cross. At any point, He could have walked away from the cross.

I believe our salvation was at its point of greatest jeopardy when Satan, through the voices of mortal men, taunted and mocked Jesus, saying, "He saved others," they said, "but he can't save himself! He's the king of Israel! Let him come down now from the cross, and we will believe in him" (Matthew 27:42). This dual temptation of seeking relief from pain and suffering and appealing to the pride of humanity that demands to be respected must have been almost more than Jesus could bear.

It is a good thing that all of humanity was not dependent upon me for its salvation, because in that moment I have no doubt what I would have done. I would have come down from the cross, showing my power immediately. I would have come down with a full demonstration of my power by giving the command to wipe out every mocker in my sight. I would have come down from that cross in plain sight of everyone present to display once and for all that I, indeed, was the King of Kings. I would have quit. But Jesus never quits.

Not once during the entire grueling ordeal did Jesus exercise the option to abandon the mission. The Garden of Gethsemane alone would have been enough to weed out most people, if not all. It is interesting to note that the Garden of Gethsemane means "garden of pressing." It is the place where, once picked, olives would be taken to have the juices pressed out of them. It was there, in that garden where the horrors of the cross and the dreaded separation from His eternal, holy Father caused Jesus such emotional and mental pressure, that His life's blood was literally pressed out of His veins through the pores of His skin as great drops of blood, mixed with sweat, spilled onto the ground. Yet Jesus didn't quit.

He didn't quit when He grew tired from being up all night, marching from one kangaroo court to the next. He didn't quit when the Jewish officials slapped Him across the face. He didn't quit when the Roman soldiers struck Him with the backs of their hands, their closed fists, and their wooden clubs. He didn't quit when blow after blow caused His eyes and lips to swell and bleed, disfiguring His face and swelling His head as He was struck again and again and again. He didn't quit when He saw those same soldiers fashioning a

crown of thorns He knew would be placed on His head. He didn't quit when that crown, whose thorns were up to five inches long, was pressed brutally into His beaten brow, piercing His skin and skull.

He didn't quit as His hands were being tied to the flogging post and a fearful expectation of the 39 lashes He was about to receive, no doubt, rose up within Him, consuming His imagination. He didn't quit at the sight of the chiseled, muscular Roman executioner picking up the whip whose end was shredded into nine strips of leather, each strip embedded with shards of iron, bone, and sharpened stones that would inflict the most dreadful of lacerations all over the back of His body. He didn't quit when that first lash sank deep into the flesh on His shoulders, back, and legs. He didn't quit when that Roman soldier, with a flick of his well-trained wrist and a mighty heave of his strong arm ripped the cat-of-nine-tails along His back, tearing out pieces of skin, flesh, and muscle. He didn't quit the whipping post, even though the bleeding through His pores the night before in the Garden of Gethsemane made His skin that much more sensitive and tender to the touch, heightening and intensifying the sting of each agonizing lash.

Rather than quitting, He endured lash, after lash, after lash, after lash, after lash...thirty-nine of them in all. How long does it take to administer thirty-nine lashes? It must have seemed a hair's breadth short of eternity to Jesus. Yet Jesus didn't quit. Not after lash 8, lash 13, lash 17, lash 22, lash 27, lash 31, lash 32, lash 37, lash 38, or lash 39. Thirty-nine lashes. One lash short of the number that executioners believed would be fatal. The pain of this severe and prolonged beating would have been enough to cause Jesus to fade in and out of consciousness, but it wasn't enough to cause Him to quit. He didn't quit; knowing the worst of His agony still lay directly ahead.

He didn't quit at the sight of His captors bringing the wooden crossbeam to be placed squarely on the fresh wounds across His bloody shoulders. He didn't quit when they forced Him to carry this heavy burden along a narrow, winding path of crowded streets—streets filled with gawking, ridiculing onlookers spitting on and punching His distorted, bleeding face. He didn't quit when the sleepless night, long marches, emotional distress, inhumane thrashing, and considerable loss of blood all combined to cause Him to stumble and fall beneath the pressing weight of the cross. He didn't quit when Simon the Cyrene was enlisted to help Him carry that cross up Calvary's hill, where His greatest torment still awaited, the hill where He would face a burden that He alone was strong enough to bear—a burden no one else could help Him carry.

He didn't quit when each pain-ridden step filled Him with an ever-increasing sense of doom and despair as He drew closer to the top of that hill known as Golgotha, the "place of the skull." He didn't quit when, no doubt more than once, the passage "He was pierced for our transgressions" (Isaiah 53:5) passed through His mind, overwhelming Him with a fearful apprehension of what was to come. Nor did He quit when, upon cresting the summit of that mount, He turned to see, for the first time, the implements of His execution.

The Romans had learned in their long history of executions that the horror of seeing the cross, the hammer, and the nails would often cause the convicted criminals to begin frantically resisting the Roman soldiers' efforts to drive the iron spikes through their arms and feet, pinning them to the tree where they would die a slow and agonizing death.

Growing weary of fighting the prisoners at this point, as a matter of convenience, the Romans made it a practice to separate both of the prisoner's shoulders, rendering the prisoner incapable of resisting the guards, making it much easier to nail the convicted criminal to the cross.

How shocked the Romans must have been when Jesus, without any resistance, freely and willingly laid Himself down onto that bed of wood and, apart from any direction or order, voluntarily spread His arms across the beam to be pierced for our transgressions. Rest assured, no muscular Roman soldier overpowered Christ that day, forcing Him to yield, because no man could take the life of Jesus. He laid it down freely. Yet despite this willingness on the part of Jesus to subject Himself to His crucifixion, in keeping with tradition, the Roman soldiers dislocated both of His shoulders, pulling them from their joints. Still, Jesus did not quit.

He didn't quit when He felt the pain of those spikes being hammered through each wrist. He didn't quit from the incommunicable pain He felt as each spike was driven through the most tender part of each foot. He didn't quit when wave after wave of unspeakable pain would shoot through His body as each strike of the hammer drove those nails deeper and deeper through Him, into the wood, pinching Him to the cross. A more brutal form of execution has never been conceived in the mind of men. Yet even this fiercest mode of death was not enough to cause Jesus to quit.

Having been nailed to the wood of the cross, He didn't quit when that cross was slowly raised from a horizontal position to an upright, vertical position where Jesus would hang between heaven and earth, where that cross would then be dropped into a hole about three feet deep. He didn't quit for fear of the intense pain that would accompany the mighty jolt of being dropped into that hole, gravity ruthlessly jerking His body against the spikes upon which He was hanging.

I can remember the first roller coaster I ever rode when I was a young boy. It was a very simple roller coaster—nothing more than a slow ride up a steep incline, an equally slow right turn at the top, followed by what then seemed to be a death-defying drop back down to the bottom, where a jarring right turn would begin the slow, fearful journey back up to the top of the roller coaster all over again. This cycle repeated for about four or five laps. I was too young at the time to appreciate the thrill of the roller coaster. I was terrified of the quick drop, the sense of losing control during the free fall, and the whipping and jerking action going into the right turn at the bottom.

I distinctly remember every aspect of that ride. I remember the eerie sensation of my stomach rising into my chest as we plummeted straight down toward the ground. I remember being slammed into the left door as the car banked sharply into the right turn. I remember the sudden jerk and the clackety-clack-clack-clack sounds at the end of that turn as the cars latched onto the hooks in the chain that carried us back up that long, slow journey into the sky. I remember how my fear and anxiety would escalate after every cha-chink, cha-chink, cha-chink the cars made as we rose higher and higher, my fearful anticipation of the soon-coming fall growing continually until I could stand it no longer and I would scream at the top of my lungs: "Make them stop, Mom! Make them stop! I want to get off...I want to get off!" But the ride wasn't over.

I remember that experience often when I think of Christ being raised on the cross—a fearful expectation rising within Him of the great pain He would feel when the cross came crashing to an abrupt halt at the end of that three-foot drop, His body yanking against the spikes nailing Him to the cross. I wonder if at that time, while being slowly raised to a vertical position, there wasn't the voice of a scared little boy somewhere deep inside Jesus crying out, "Make them stop, Father! Make them stop! I want to get off...I want to get off!" But Jesus didn't quit.

When that cross came crashing down with a sickening thud, gravity tugging mercilessly against the spikes that pinned Him to that tree, Jesus may have let out a scream of agony that shook the gates of hell and echoed in the chambers of heaven, but Jesus didn't quit. The ride wasn't over.

For Jesus, it was just beginning. All the cruelty He experienced before the crucifixion—the beatings, the flogging, the crown of thorns, the cat-of-nine-tails, carrying the cross up the hill, the nails—was designed for one purpose: to increase the suffering Jesus experienced while on the cross.

The cross was designed to make the most basic and necessary of life's functions—breathing—a constant source of grievous torture. The combination of extending Jesus' arms to the point of separation from the shoulders, while at the same time drawing His feet up under His knees, and nailing Him in this position caused the full weight of His body to pull down and apart on His chest cavity, leaving it in a perpetually expanded state. In this position, His chest could neither fall to exhale nor rise to inhale. To breathe, Jesus would have to push up on the spike in His feet while pulling on the nails in His hands in order to reach a point where His chest cavity could rise and fall so that normal respiration could occur.

Try to imagine the sensation of Christ hanging by two nails on the cross, wrists and separated shoulders throbbing with pain, His body screaming for more oxygen than His shallow breathing would allow. Imagine the cruelty of His having to indulge the pleasure of a full breath at the pain of pushing against the spike run through the most tender part of both feet, while at the same time, pulling on the nails in both wrists, increasing the intense pain in both separated shoulders. Imagine the pain of the raw, open wounds from the 39 lashings that shredded His back grating against the coarse, splintered wood as He pushed and pulled Himself up and down against the cross to draw each pain-filled breath.

Imagine the agony of Jesus drawing a few, heavily-labored breaths from this elevated position, the pain of bone-on-iron contact in His feet eventually becoming intolerable, forcing Him to lower Himself back down on the cross, transferring pain from a concentrated, single point in His feet, back up His body to both shoulders and the spikes in each wrist. Imagine relieving the pain in His feet only at the cost of reviving the pain pulsing through each arm and separated shoulder, while simultaneously reviving the discomfort of asphyxiation from this hanging position. Imagine Jesus, unable to stand the oxygen deprivation any longer, having to repeat the same grueling process all over again. How many reps of this painful exercise could you endure before quitting? Is there any workout routine or aerobics class to compare? Yet Jesus endured this agonizing exercise for six hours. Six hours, and He never quit.

Jesus didn't quit when the crown of thorns pierced His skin anew each time His face grimaced, giving expression to His immense suffering. He didn't quit from the overwhelming pain in His neck from hanging His head down and out in an extended position for six hours, because the weight of His head resting on the cross would only push the thorns in the crown deeper into His skull.

No relief could be found in any position on the cross, only a constant bombardment of severe pain from every part of His body—each part crying out for, screaming for, vying for His attention— demanding to be relieved from its torture, relief coming in one area only at the expense of greater agony in another, a constant battle between the pain of death and the pain of sustaining life, life that would only prolong this misery and torment.

Of all the things that were causing Him pain and anguish, none were sufficient to warrant either a complaint or a mention, save the desire to satiate His great thirst.

Jesus suffered ridicule, abuse, disrespect, the shame of public nakedness, beatings, bruising, impalement, traumatic head injury, rejection, betrayal, abandonment, the sting of being punctured, the pain of receiving nauseating blows with blunt objects, asphyxiation, and thirst.

Throughout the crucifixion there were seven recorded sayings of Jesus. Only two were in reference to Himself, one of which was the saying, "I thirst" (John 19:28 KJV). Think about that. Of all the things that were causing Him pain and anguish, none were sufficient to warrant either a complaint or a mention, save the desire to satiate His great thirst. How great a thirst that must have been. That statement reveals that in His death, Jesus suffered all the consequences and curses of sin. The thorns the earth produced as a result of the curse mentioned in Genesis were placed upon the head of Jesus. The blood of the animal that was first shed to provide the clothing God made for Adam and Eve foretold of the blood Christ would shed on the cross as He once again dressed mankind in the clothes of righteousness made by His life and death. The requirement to be stoned for transgressing the law was experienced by Christ in the many close-fisted blows to the face and head He received at the hands of the Jewish community. The threat of being torn apart as the animal of the covenant was torn apart can be pictured in the tearing and ripping of Christ's beard from His face on the way to Calvary. The most severe

consequence of sin, the consequence of being separated from God, is seen in Jesus' questioning why God had forsaken Him—without a doubt the most traumatic of all His experiences. And while hanging on the cross, Jesus experienced the same torment the rich man experienced in Hades. Thirst.

There are times while speaking when, due to extreme nervousness, my mouth will become debilitatingly dry, causing my lips and cheeks to cling to my teeth and my tongue to cling to the roof of my mouth, making it almost impossible to speak. I must labor a great deal to get my mouth and tongue to form the vowel and consonant sounds required for speech. How much more difficult it must have been for Jesus to utter His statements, facing both the obstacles of a dried, parched mouth with a cleaving, swollen tongue, and the lack of breath necessary to speak at an audible level. We must never forget what it cost Jesus to intercede on our behalf. While His executioners and detractors stood at the foot of the cross, gawking at and insulting Him, Jesus mustered all of His remaining strength, endured the pain of pushing Himself up the cross another time, drew a painful breath, and with a swollen tongue cried out, "Father, forgive them, for they do not know what they are doing" (Luke 23:34).

Jesus cried mercy, but not for Himself. In fact, mercy was why Jesus was on the cross. Jesus was on the cross to suffer the consequences of sin in our place, so that we could enjoy the blessings of righteousness in His place. While Jesus was on the cross, God the Father was pouring out His wrath for the sins of all mankind on the sinless Christ. On the cross, Jesus was paying the price for our sins, and only when the last sin had been paid for, only after every last drop of God's indignation had been poured out on Jesus, did He finally exclaim, "Father, into Your hands I commit My Spirit" (Luke 23:46). God completed His work of creation in six days, Christ Jesus completed His work of redemption in six hours. Then, and only then, when His work of redemption was complete, did Jesus finally and triumphantly cry, "It is finished" (John 19:30). Then, and only then, did Jesus give up His Spirit. Until the job was finished, Jesus never quit.

Oh, listen, my friend! If there was ever a time Jesus would have quit on you, it would have been on the cross. But Jesus didn't quit on you at Calvary, and He's not going to quit on you now! Jesus never quits!

Chapter 4:
Jesus Never Leaves a Fallen Comrade

The mission Jesus placed first was rescuing us from our fallen condition. He did this by making a way of salvation to God for us. One way. Many people believe the false statement that God is like a mountain with many paths leading to the same summit. God is not like a mountain. God is like a Garth Brooks concert.

When Garth Brooks came to my hometown of Evansville, Indiana, he created quite a stir. He was to perform at Roberts Municipal Stadium. The problem was there were more Garth Brooks fans than stadium seats. They solved this problem in two ways: multiple concerts and a lottery. Country music stations broadcast detailed instructions over the airwaves that had to be strictly adhered to if you wanted to see Garth Brooks. If you wished to attend one of his concerts, you had to go to one of a few specific locations to get a plastic wristband. On this wristband was printed a number. Your number. A lottery was then held in which a random number was drawn. If the number drawn matched the number printed on your wristband, you were the lucky person to get first in line to buy Garth Brooks tickets. Everyone else then fell in line behind you in numerical order, beginning with the next number higher than yours. People then bought tickets in numerical order until every last ticket was sold.

This process did not appeal to me. It was inconvenient and time consuming, and there were no guarantees I would get a ticket. The location wasn't close by, I didn't want to stand in line, and quite honestly, I couldn't afford the tickets anyway. Still, given the situation, it was the fairest way possible of dealing with the problem of having more fans than seats.

Now imagine another radio station coming on the air and saying, "That is not a good way to sell tickets. If you want, you just call our station, and we will sell them to you over the telephone." Or another station saying,

"Well, that is not how I interpreted the promoter's instructions. What their instructions mean to me is that all you need to do is get the wristband, and the number printed on the band is your seat number in the stadium." Imagine another station saying, "Garth Brooks is a good guy who loves all of his fans. If you just show up the night of the concert, you will get a seat. They will make room for you. Don't worry about all of that wristband business. What a hassle." They could have said all that, but they would have all been wrong because they would not have been speaking on the authority of the promoters. To follow any instructions other than what Garth's people had given would have left you outside in the cold, unable to get in, because your beliefs, no matter how sincere, would not have matched reality.

The problem with heaven is not a space problem; it is a sin problem.

That is how it is with heaven, with one major exception. The problem with heaven is not a space problem; it is a sin problem. Sin is the problem that keeps people out

of heaven, and there is only one solution to that problem: Jesus.

People have a general misconception of how intolerant God is toward sin. With us, there is an acceptable level of failure. We are comfortable with sin. "To err is human," right? But any such comfort with or tolerance toward sin is unacceptable to a holy God. The Bible says, "The wages of sin is death," not the wages of sins is death. Adam and Eve did not enjoy a three-strikes-and-you're-out policy. It took only one bite of the forbidden fruit for them to be expelled from the garden.

"Be perfect, therefore, as your heavenly Father is perfect" (Matthew 5:48).

With God, the standard, the requirement, is perfection. God's Word says, "Be perfect, therefore, as your heavenly Father is perfect" (Matthew 5:48). This seems a bit unrealistic to most of us. After all, who among us is perfect? We don't understand how a loving God could have such unrealistic expectations.

But is that expectation really unrealistic? Is it unrealistic to expect a restaurant to offer an omelet without any rotten eggs? If you were served an omelet with a rotten egg, would it matter that there were many good eggs in the omelet? Would it matter that the cheese, the tomatoes, the ham, the bacon, or the bell peppers were all good? No. Emphatically no. Regardless of how many good ingredients were added to that omelet, they would not make good the one rotten egg. That omelet would not be acceptable to you. It would, however, be perfectly acceptable to maggots in the Dumpster. If you were to throw that omelet away, those varmints would instantly begin devouring that entree because they are of a different nature than we are.

The moment we fail and fall short of this standard, the result is death-death being the immediate and eternal separation from God in this life, hell in the next!

So it is with our lives. While we might be comfortable with sin, God is not comfortable with sin because God is holy and therefore of a different nature than ours. He cannot tolerate sin, because He has no stomach for it. God's nature toward sin is recorded in Habakkuk 1:13:

> "Thou art of purer eyes than to behold evil, and canst not look on iniquity" (KJV).

Because of our sin, our lives are unacceptable to God regardless of how many good deeds our lives might consist of, because those good deeds cannot undo the sins that are so repulsive to a holy God. God's standard is perfection. The moment we fail and fall short of this standard, the result is death-death being the immediate and eternal separation from God in this life, hell in the next!

Hell is an absolute, irreversible, eternally hopeless existence spent enduring the wrath of a holy God. A holy God who never grows weary. A holy God whose hatred for sin and His enemies never diminishes...ever.

If you have ever had a relationship where the sheer contempt of another toward you never seems to diminish but instead appears to increase over time, with nothing you can do to change their attitude or disposition toward you, you have experienced an infinitesimally small taste of what hell is going to be

like. When those people in your life who seem to never grow weary of expressing their disgust take every opportunity to vent their frustrations or hurl their disdain toward you, you experience a minor hell on earth.

I can remember times during boot camp when our drill sergeants would subject us to grueling periods of "corrective training." After committing some error or failing to meet the ever-important standard in some area, we would often hear the words "get down and beat your face," which was their way of telling us, ever so affectionately, to do push-ups.

"Keep pushin', I'm not tired yet!"

After seemingly endless repetitions when we were at the point of complete muscle failure and exhaustion, the drill sergeant would scream, "Keep pushin', I'm not tired yet!" All of us have, at one time or another, incited the rage or incurred the wrath of another that never seemed to diminish, yet over time, their indignation gradually subsided, as they eventually grew tired of being upset with us. Such is not the case with the

Almighty. When the damned reach their moment of exhaustion from judgment, the impenitent will have nothing to look forward to but an eternity of bearing the full weight of the fury of God. The omniscience of God will be employed to bring about every conceivable form of agony, while His omnipotence will provide the never-ending force and power to carry out the just, eternal execution of wrath their sin deserves. Though hell's captives will have been punished well beyond their ability to bear and will have long since reached their point of exhaustion, yet will they hear God say, "I'm not tired yet." I can say it no better than Jonathan Edwards in Sinners in the Hands of an Angry God. I will let him speak.

> "Consider this, you that are here present, that yet remain in an unregenerate state. That God will execute the fierceness of his anger, implies, that he will inflict wrath without any pity. When God beholds the ineffable extremity of your case, and sees your torment to be so vastly disproportional to your strength, and sees how your poor soul is crushed, and sinks down, as it were, into an infinite gloom; he will have no compassion upon you, he will not forbear the executions of his wrath, or in the least lighten

his hand; there shall be no moderation or mercy, nor will God then at all stay his rough wind; he will have no regard to your welfare, nor be at all careful lest you should suffer too much in any other sense, than only that you shall not suffer beyond what strict justice requires. Nothing shall be withheld, because it is so hard for you to bear. Ezekiel 8:18. 'Therefore will I also deal in fury: mine eye shall not spare, neither will I have pity; and though they cry in mine ears with a loud voice, yet I will not hear them.'...

And though he will know that you cannot bear the weight of omnipotence treading upon you, yet he will not regard that, but he will crush you under his feet without mercy... He will not only hate you, but he will have you in the utmost contempt...It would be dreadful to suffer this fierceness and wrath of Almighty God one moment; but you must suffer it to all eternity. There will be no end to this exquisite horrible misery. When you look forward, you shall see a long for ever, a boundless duration before you, which will swallow up your thoughts, and amaze your soul; and you will absolutely despair of

> ever having any deliverance, any end, any mitigation, any rest at all. You will know certainly that you must wear out long ages, millions of millions of ages, in wrestling and conflicting with this almighty merciless vengeance; and then when you have so done, when so many ages have actually been spent by you in this manner, you will know that all is but a point to what remains. So that your punishment will indeed be infinite. Oh, who can express what the state of a soul in such circumstances is!"

Such would have been the state of each of us had Jesus not come to bear in His body the fearful blows of an angry God, experiencing for us the sting of death our sins deserved.

To think that God despises sin to such a degree that He would be pleased to bruise His only Son should strike fear in the heart of every impenitent sinner.

Some would deny that a God of love is capable of such hatred, wrath, and indignation for sin. Those people do not have a true understanding of the holiness of God. There is a startling verse in Isaiah that vividly portrays the degree to which God hates sin. Referring to Christ on the cross, Isaiah 53:10 reads, "Yet it pleased the LORD to bruise Him" (emphasis mine KJV). This verse should give us pause to consider God's attitude toward sin. To think that God despises sin to such a degree that He would be pleased to bruise His only Son should strike fear in the heart of every impenitent sinner. The fact that God's vengeance for sin was not tempered or mitigated by His own Son bearing the full weight of His fury should cause every person to see how much God hates sin, motivating him to run to the shelter of God's love and offer of forgiveness in Christ. For if God did not relent in punishing sin when that sin was placed on His own innocent Son, if God did not "pull any punches" at the pitiful sight of His only begotten writhing in agony, how much less will He relent or show pity to unrepentant sinners who are His enemies? If God did not show any mercy to His sinless, spotless Son when punishing sin, how much less will He be merciful to those who reject Christ's amazing sacrifice, who continue to sin willfully? How can those who are by nature objects of God's wrath avoid anything but,

> "A terrifying expectation of judgment and the fury of a fire which will consume the adversaries...It is a terrifying thing to fall into the hands of the living God" (Hebrews 10:27, 32).

Jesus Himself alluded to the horrors of hell in the parable of the Rich Man and Lazarus. After the rich man died he awoke in Hades, instantly conscious of being in great torment. He found himself in the grip of an indescribable thirst, wanting nothing more than the smallest drop of water applied to his hot, dried, parched tongue—a tongue withered by the unquenchable flames and relentless fires of hell. Though he sought for relief with all his heart, there was none to be found.

Sin bears such horrid consequences because sin is such a horrid act. When we sin, we call into question the wisdom, the goodness, and the power of God. When faced with a choice between several options, we make our choice based upon which option we believe will have the most desirable outcome. Whenever we choose an option that God has expressly forbidden or fail to take the option that God has commanded, we are making the statement that our option is more

desirable than the option God has commanded. By our choices we are stating that God does not know what is best, therefore insulting His intelligence; God knows what is best but is intentionally keeping us from it, thereby insulting His character and goodness; and/or regardless of what God knows or how much He cares, we are going to do whatever we want with complete disregard for His power to discipline or execute judgment, because we don't think He can do anything about it, therefore insulting His power. We insult His power because we don't believe that He can exact consequences sufficient to make our choices any less desirable. We show complete contempt for His position and authority. There is no fear of God before our eyes. Whenever we commit these egregious offenses against an eternal God, we incur an eternal debt that requires an eternity to pay.

Jesus' death alone is sufficient to pay that eternal debt, because only Jesus is Himself eternal and because only Jesus is Himself eternally sinless. We know that Jesus is sinless because the resurrection validates the sinlessness of Christ. If Jesus had sinned during His lifetime, He would have remained in the grave, unresurrected, having received the just punishment for His sin—death. If He had not been resurrected, His death would have proved that He had sinned and was therefore under the same curse that befalls everyone who sins, the curse of death. His unresurrected death would have proven that He deserved to die just as everyone else, because He had sinned just like everyone else and was therefore human just like everyone else. But Jesus did not sin like everyone else. He did not remain in the grave like everyone else. He was not human like everyone else. Unlike others, He arose from the grave under His own power. Jesus died because He took our sin upon Himself and experienced the consequences of our sin for us—death. Jesus arose from death because He Himself was sinless and therefore did not deserve to die. Death could not keep Him in the grave. His death proved that He paid the price for the sins of humanity, while His resurrection proved He was Himself without sin. His resurrection proves that our sins have been forgiven. His resurrection proves that Jesus was not just human but divine as well.

His executioners and detractors denied the divinity of Christ, believing Jesus was human only. His enemies believed His claims of deity were tantamount to blasphemy. When Jesus told the paralytic, "Your sins are forgiven" (Matthew 9:2), the Pharisees asked,

"Who can forgive sins but God alone?" (Mark 2:7). This is a valid question. Only the person who is owed a debt can forgive the debt. Would an account manager for Visa be able to write off a debt owed to MasterCard? Absolutely not! When Jesus declared the sins of the paralytic forgiven, He claimed for Himself the authority to forgive sins, an authority the Pharisees rightly identified as an authority belonging to God alone. An authority they denied Jesus having. Aware of their thoughts Jesus asked in Mark 2:8-9:

> "Why are you thinking these things? Which is easier: to say to the paralytic, 'Your sins are forgiven,' or to say, 'Get up, take your mat and walk'?"

The answer to that rhetorical question is "They are both equally difficult, both equally miraculous; therefore, both equally something God alone could do." To prove to the disbelieving Pharisees that He indeed had the authority to forgive sins and was therefore equal with God, Jesus said in Mark 2:10-12:

> "But that you may know that the Son of Man has authority on earth to forgive sins...." He said to the paralytic, "I tell you, get up, take your mat

> and go home." He got up, took his mat and walked out in full view of them all. This amazed everyone, and they praised God, saying, "We have never seen anything like this!"

Despite this miraculous display of power and authority, the Pharisees persisted in their disbelief. This rejection of the divinity and sinlessness of Christ by the religious leaders of Jesus' day reaches its climax during the kangaroo trial held by the Sanhedrin prior to the crucifixion of Jesus. After a few conflicting testimonies by false witnesses, the patience of Caiaphas, the high priest, grows thin, and he demands of Jesus:

> "I charge you under oath by the living God: Tell us if you are the Christ, the Son of God."
>
> "Yes, it is as you say," Jesus replied. "But I say to all of you: In the future you will see the Son of Man sitting at the right hand of the mighty one and coming on the clouds of heaven."
>
> Then the high priest tore his clothes and said, "He has spoken blasphemy! Why do we need any more witnesses? Look, now you have heard the blasphemy. What do you think?" "He

> is worthy of death," they answered. (Matthew 26:63-66)

Rather than evaluating His claims of deity, they equated His claims with blasphemy. Rather than worship Him as God, they whipped Him as a sinner. Rather than crown Him as king, they crucified Him as a criminal. But even in their evil actions, they were unwitting participants in the divine plan of God to make a way of salvation for all mankind. For it was through this death that He would pay for the sins of humanity, providing ultimate proof for His claim to deity.

It is easy to make claims, difficult to deliver on them. To up the ante on His claims of divinity and sinlessness, Jesus foretold His greatest miracle and affirmation yet. As recorded in the Gospel of John, Jesus is asked by the Jewish leaders:

> "What miraculous sign can you show us to prove your authority to do all this?" Jesus answered them, "Destroy this temple, and I will raise it again in three days." The Jews replied, "It has taken forty-six years to build this temple, and you are going to raise it in three days?" But

> the temple he had spoken of was his body. (John 2:18-21)

He also said:

> “For as Jonah was three days and three nights in the belly of a huge fish, so the Son of Man will be three days and three nights in the heart of the earth.” (Matthew 12:40)

The Gospel of Matthew records this:

> He then began to teach them that the Son of Man must suffer many things and be rejected by the elders, chief priests and teachers of the law, and that he must be killed and after three days rise again. He spoke plainly about this, he said to them, “The Son of Man is going to be betrayed into the hands of men. They will kill him, and on the third day he will be raised to life”
> (Matthew 17:22).

Even the enemies of Jesus were aware of these predictions as recorded in Matthew:

> The next day, the one after Preparation Day, the chief priests and the Pharisees went to Pilate. "Sir," they said, "we remember that while he was still alive that deceiver said, 'After three days I will rise again.'" (Matthew 27:62-63)

Read what happened next to "that deceiver":

> On the evening of that first day of the week, when the disciples were together, with the doors locked for fear of the Jews, Jesus came and stood among them and said, "Peace be with you!" After he said this, he showed them his hands and side. The disciples were overjoyed when they saw the Lord.
> Again Jesus said, "Peace be with you!" (John 20:19-21)

> Now Thomas (called Didymus), one of the Twelve, was not with the disciples when Jesus came. So the other disciples told him, "We have seen the Lord!"
> But he said to them, "Unless I see the nail marks in his hands and put my finger where the nails were, and put my hand into his side, I will not believe it."

> A week later his disciples were in the house again, and Thomas was with them. Though the doors were locked, Jesus came and stood among them and said, "Peace be with you!" Then he said to Thomas, "Put your finger here; see my hands. Reach out your hand and put it into my side. Stop doubting and believe." Thomas said to him, "My Lord and my God!" Then Jesus told him, "Because you have seen me, you have believed; blessed are those who have not seen and yet have believed." (John 20:24-29)

The resurrection and appearances to His disciples are the ultimate proofs of His divinity and the efficacious atonement for the sins of man.

It was His perfect, sinless life that made Him rich enough in the currency of heaven to pay the debt we owed for our sin.

Sin must be punished. God's holiness and justice will not allow sin to go unpunished. He won't just write off

the sin debt. There are only two options: the guilty will receive the eternal hell their sins justly deserve or someone perfectly innocent and sinless will be punished on behalf of the guilty. Jesus left His throne in glory, came to earth as a man, and lived the perfectly sinless life that was needed to be the satisfactory, substitutionary sacrifice. He paid the sin-debt mankind owed by suffering the death mankind deserved, satisfied the righteous requirements of the law, satiated the wrath of God against sin, and secured a means of forgiveness for humanity. A trade occurred at Calvary. Jesus took our sin and gave us His righteousness. Jesus, who had no sin, took our sin upon Himself and experienced the death we deserved, in our stead. Jesus who was rich in righteousness, spent that righteousness on us, becoming poor so that we in our impoverished state of sin might be made rich through His righteousness. It was His perfect, sinless life that made Him rich enough in the currency of heaven to pay the debt we owed for our sin.

This is why Jesus is the way, the truth, and the life, and why no man can come unto the Father but through Him. This is why there is no other name under heaven by which men shall be saved. There is no other person under heaven that was, is, or ever will be perfectly righteous. There is, therefore, no other person rich enough in the currency of heaven to pay the sin debt that you and I and all of humanity owed. Every other religious leader falls into the category of "all have sinned and fall short of the glory of God"(Romans 3:23); therefore every other religious leader is bankrupt in righteousness. Every other religious system fails to deal sufficiently with the problem of sin. A system that is bankrupt and a person who is bankrupt cannot possibly pay off the sin debt of another. They have no resources to pay the debt. No other religious leader or system can circumvent the perfect righteousness that God's holiness requires. There is no way to please a holy God but through perfection. Rather than bemoan the God of holiness for the perfection His justice demands, bestow praise upon that same God of love for His marvelous gift of grace that allowed the sinless Christ to suffer death on our behalf to satisfy His holy justice. Praise God that His justice makes no further demands upon us.

If we will confess our sins, seek His forgiveness, cease from our futile striving, and rest in this finished work of Christ on the cross, God will, by the sacrifice of Jesus, make each and every one of us acceptable to Him. All who call upon the name of the Lord shall be saved.

To complain of having only one option for salvation is like flood victims on a chimney top complaining to the rescuers in a boat who are risking their lives to save them, because the flood victims would rather be rescued by a helicopter! Quit complaining, be thankful, and get in the boat!

For those who claim that God would not restrict forgiveness, restoration, and eternal life to just one path, I ask, “Then why would Jesus have died on the cross?” If it were possible to get to heaven by any other religion or all other religions, then why would Jesus have suffered so much? If a means of salvation could be made apart from Jesus’ death, burial, and resurrection, why would He have endured the agonies of Calvary? Why wouldn’t Jesus just say, “I’m not going through with this crucifixion thing. If people want to get to heaven, let them become a _____________ (fill in blank), or let them follow whateverism. I’m not going through this torture.” In fact, Jesus Himself sought to be spared the whole horrible ordeal of the cross when He fell on His face to the ground in the Garden of Gethsemane and prayed:

> "My Father, if it is possible, let this cup pass from Me; yet not as I will, but as You will." (Matthew 26:39)

But the cup did not pass from Him, because there was no other way to secure forgiveness for the sins of mankind. Only the sinless life of Christ crucified on the cross can pay for and eliminate our sin debt, wash away all of our sins, and restore us to a right relationship with God.

Having sinned, we could do nothing to undo that sin. We were forever marred with the stain of sin's imperfection, and that stain could never and would never be removed through any human effort. That is why Jesus Himself said, "I am the way, the truth and the life; no man comes unto the Father but by Me" (John 14:6). What a blessed comfort to know that our sins have been forgiven and that we have been cleansed from all of our iniquity because the innocent Jesus suffered the consequences of our guilt on our behalf. Marvelous grace indeed!

Grace is the single mark of distinction that separates Christianity from every other religion. Christianity and the world's religions can be likened to two Old

Testament pictures. The first is the image of the Tower of Babel with its stairway intended to reach the throne of heaven—a tower built by man that represents man's attempt to reach God through his own power and

Christianity is the faith that says, "If I am to make it to heaven, it will not be because I did it my way, or because I earned my way, or because I made a way, but because heaven has descended and made a way for me!"

works. The second is that of Jacob's ladder—a ladder that in Jacob's dream originated in heaven and reached down to earth, a ladder not made by human hands, a ladder with angels ascending and descending upon it. Of these two pictures, Christianity is the picture of Jacob's ladder. Christianity is the faith that says, "If I am to make it to heaven, it will not be because I did it my way, or because I earned my way, or because I made a way, but because heaven has descended and made a way for me!"

> For it is by grace you have been saved, through faith—and this not from yourselves, it is the gift of God—not by works, so that no one can boast. (Ephesians 2:8-9)

Perhaps an illustration would aptly portray the gospel. In many ways, heaven is like the PGA tour in golf. In golf, the aim is to get the ball in the cup. The cup is the goal, the mark. With each hole, there is an acceptable level of goal-missing, or mark-missing, known as par. On a par 5 hole, you can miss the cup, or the mark if you will, five times, and still be acceptable. To qualify for the PGA tour, you cannot exceed the acceptable standard of mark-missing but must consistently shoot under par. This is why I wish the PGA tour was one big best-ball tournament. A best-ball tournament is an adaptation of the game of golf. A best-ball tournament is a four-person team effort in which the team's score is determined by the score of the teammate who gets the ball in the cup in the fewest strokes. If the four members of the team shot a 6, 5, 8, and 3 on a particular hole, the team would receive a score of 3 for that hole, because the score of the individual who played that hole best (3) is attributed to the entire team. I wish the PGA were one big best-ball tournament, because I will never be good enough to qualify on my own ability. If the PGA were a best-ball tournament, I wouldn't have to be good enough to qualify, I would just have to convince Tiger Woods to let me play on his team. Then, and only then, would I qualify, because when the judges looked at my scorecard, all they would see is Tiger Woods' score. My score would be determined by his play.

With heaven, par is not 5 or 4 or even 3 for a particular hole, but because God is holy, par is and must be 1. Every shot in life must be a hole-in-one. The moment you miss the mark, which is the very definition of sin, by the way, you are forever disqualified from entering heaven. Since no one is perfect, no one is going to qualify for heaven based upon their own efforts. That is why I am so grateful that heaven is one big best-ball tournament. Jesus came to earth and for 33 years lived a sinless life. For 33 years he shot a perfect 18, every day. He then died on the cross, suffered the consequences our sin deserved so that sin would be punished in Him on our behalf, and satisfied God's righteous requirements for sin to be punished. He in essence paid the entry fee for our participation in the PGA tournament in heaven. He now invites all who would like to play on His team to be listed on His scorecard. If you would confess your sins, seek His forgiveness, and surrender to His Lordship, He offers the opportunity for your name to be placed on His scorecard so that when God looks at your name, He won't see your sin, but He'll see Christ's perfect 18.

A few years back, then-governor of Minnesota Jesse Ventura made the comment that Christianity was a crutch for the weak. Many, many Christians took offense at these comments. I'm not sure why. Governor Ventura was absolutely correct. I am weak in my own strength, yea, more than weak, powerless. I, like the paralytic in the Gospel of Mark, was crippled with sin, crushed under the great weight of the eternal debt that my imperfections imposed. The burden of sin paralyzed me, rendering me completely incapable of taking any steps toward forgiveness or heaven. But then, some friends of my parents took me to Jesus, and through the preaching of His Word, He spoke words of forgiveness and healing toward me. Because Jesus satisfied the debt for my sin on the cross, He now offers that cross to me as a crutch whereby I am made able to walk toward a new life in Him. It is with this crutch of the cross and because of that cross that I will one day walk through the gates of heaven. So I am in complete agreement with Governor Ventura—Christianity is a crutch for the weak. And I would rather

hobble into heaven leaning on the crutch of the cross of Christ than go bounding through the gates of eternal hell on the strength of my own two legs!

The fact is, we need the crutch of the cross. We need a Savior. We need a champion to fight for us, to secure victory for us. We need Jesus who is that champion. We need Jesus who is that Warrior fighting for us, securing victory for us. We need Jesus, who is that Savior. When sin entered the world, plunging humanity into absolute and utter hopelessness and in desperate need of a Savior, Jesus descended to the occasion. When all of humanity was destined for an eternity in hell to bear the unrelenting fury of an almighty God throughout endless ages without any hope of forgiveness, Jesus left His throne in glory to stand between us and the Most High, to shield us from the anger of God, to bear the full force of God's just wrath for our sin in His own body, to pay the price for our sin, and to secure a means of forgiveness for us. Jesus did battle for us against Satan, sin, death, hell, and the grave, and three days later He arose the victor! He did all of this because "all have sinned and fall short of the glory of God" (Romans 3:23)—and Jesus never leaves a fallen comrade!

Jesus endured what He endured and suffered what He suffered because He loves us with an unspeakable love.

When Adam and Eve defied God's command by eating the forbidden fruit, they were expelled from God's presence in the Garden of Eden to a world ruled by sin and death. This expulsion is known as the Fall. The Fall steeped all humanity in sin, separating all mankind from the life and presence of God. The Fall gave rise to Jesus' descent from glory to humanity to make a way for our salvation, that we might once again walk with God in the cool of the evening in the garden of His presence. Jesus endured what He endured and suffered what He suffered because He loves us with an unspeakable love and has demonstrated "... His love toward us, in that while we were yet sinners, Christ died for us" (Romans 5:8 NASB). He died to save us from the coming wrath of God. Why did Jesus have to die for us? Because the Bible states that "all have sinned and fall short of the glory of God" and "the wages of sin is death" (Romans 6:23). To put it succinctly: you sin, you die. The apostle Paul in the

book of Romans calls this "the law of sin and death" (Romans 8:2)—death being separation from God in this life, hell in the next! People are quick to quote the Bible when it says, "God is love" (1 John 4:16) but are less likely to embrace that same Bible when it says, "Yet he does not leave the guilty unpunished" (Exodus 34:7). In essence, God loves people but hates and must punish sin. To make this proposition more personal, God loves you but hates your sin. It is your sin that separates you from God, and it is your sin that is your single greatest problem.

All other problems mentioned in this book are temporary: cancer, divorce, abuse, famine, illiteracy, inflation, war, prejudice—all terrible problems, all temporary problems, problems that will affect you no longer than your lifetime. Sin and separation from God, however, affect you forever.

This is why Jesus came to die. He came to die so that you could live forever. He came to live the perfect life that you and I could not live, to take our sin upon Himself, to suffer the consequences we deserved for our sin on our behalf as our sacrificial substitute, so that we might escape the terrible judgment of God that our sin so justly deserves. Through His sacrifice, we have forgiveness of sins and the promise of eternal life with Him in heaven. In this way, God demonstrates His hatred of sin by punishing it in His Son on the cross, while at the same time demonstrating His love toward us in allowing His Son to be sacrificed in our place so that we might have a way of salvation—salvation from the wrath of God against sin.

In time of trouble I think about Jesus being the Greatest Warrior who never leaves a fallen comrade, and I am filled with great hope because I am reminded that He who paid the greatest price to ensure that I would not remain fallen in my greatest need would never leave me fallen in my lesser needs. As the apostle Paul states in Romans 8:32:

> He who did not spare His own Son, but delivered Him over for us all, how will He not also with Him freely give us all things?

Chapter 5:
What This Means for Our Battles

Meditating on this new vision of Jesus that first, lonely, cold Sunday morning of basic training, I became overwhelmed with emotion thinking about this divine, Mighty Warrior who always placed the mission first, never accepted defeat, never quit, and never left a fallen comrade. I understood in a much clearer sense what it means that

> We do not have a high priest who is unable to sympathize with our weaknesses, but we have one who has been tempted in every way, just as we are—yet was without sin. (Hebrews 4:15)

Jesus knew what it meant to leave home, feel alone, experience rejection, bear betrayal, cope with disappointment, suffer abuse, endure poverty and hunger, confront fear, experience death, and overcome it all in victory.

The Holy Spirit began to impress upon me that Jesus went through all of that for me. I was His mission. I was the comrade He refused to leave fallen. I was the one on whom He was never going to quit, and I was the one for whom He would never accept defeat. The Holy Spirit began to impress upon me what it meant when Jesus said in John 16:33:

> "In the world you have tribulation, but take courage; I have overcome the world."

For the first time I began to realize no matter how bleak my situation, how deep the depression, how severe the loneliness, how great the pain, or how hopeless the circumstances, because Jesus overcame, I could overcome. Because Jesus overcame, I had access to the blessings of God. Because Jesus overcame, my salvation was secure. Because Jesus overcame, I had become a child of God. Because Jesus secured victory by overcoming the greatest enemies of all—sin and death—for me, He could secure any victory and overcome any enemy for me. The same is true for you.

Because Jesus overcame, you should never accept defeat. You should never accept defeat, because Jesus will never leave you fallen. Knowing Jesus will never leave you fallen means you should never quit. You should never quit because Jesus always places the mission first, and He who began the good work in you will be faithful to complete it.

I know the outlook in your life now may be so dreary that all you can see is death and despair. I know what it is to look around in every direction and not see even the slightest glimmer of hope, or life, or possibility, anywhere, literally and figuratively.

When our unit arrived in Kuwait at the beginning of our deployment, one of the first things we did was to take our weapons out to the range to make sure they functioned properly and to demonstrate the level of proficiency in marksmanship required for a combat zone. Although I do not carry a weapon as a chaplain and therefore had no need to go to the range, I accompanied the troops for support and encouragement. I had been to a few ranges before, but never one like this. I had often heard about that place known as "the middle of nowhere," and even thought that I had been there a few times, but not until that day

did I discover where nowhere really is. I'm sure we have locations like that in America; I had just never been anywhere like it until that day in Kuwait. We drove miles and miles for what seemed like forever to get to this remote part of the desert where we were to fire our weapons. When we arrived, I stepped out of the bus into the most desolate, barren wasteland I have ever seen. I was immediately struck with a sense of overwhelming insignificance. I've never felt so small. In times past, while standing at the ocean's edge looking out over the vast expanse of water and sky, I had tasted a small portion of that feeling of insignificance, dread, and fear, but any such feelings were tempered by the comfort afforded from simply turning around and observing all the welcoming and secure amenities of modern civilization available immediately behind me. There in the desert, there were no amenities behind me. It was the first time in my life where I could look 360 degrees around me and see nothing but absence. Absence of everything save the sun, sand, and sky. It was at the same time wondrous and frightful.

I couldn't help but think about what it would be like if our bus broke down and we were forced to walk the rest of the way back. Not back to where we were staying in Kuwait but to our camp in Iraq. What if we had to walk the entire journey with nothing more than what we were carrying? For the first time in my life, I felt a sense of empathy for those grumbling Israelites wandering in the desert after they had just come up out of Egypt.

As we drove out to the range that morning, I remember looking out the window in sheer and utter awe of the absolute desolation—desolation that surrounded us for as far as the eye could see. I remember thinking, How could anyone survive out here? There was nothing but a vast sea of wave after massive wave of rolling sand, undulating endlessly across the horizon, the crest of each wave greeting us only with visions of more waves of sand that continued seemingly without end. As soon as we stepped out of the bus onto the floor of that endless sandy sea, we began consuming water in great quantities. My imagination of desert wanderings began to run wild. What would become of our morale if we were to run out of water before we ran out of desert? What would become of our unit cohesion after the second or third day of trudging through desert sands in 130-plus degree heat beneath an unyielding, unrelenting, blazing sun... with no food or water? I remember thinking, We could walk for days and days and not find enough vegetation to feed just one Soldier, let alone 600. Yet there were hundreds of thousands of Israelites, perhaps millions, in that situation. While I do not condone or excuse their complaining against God, from a human perspective I can understand it. In that situation, a human perspective would accept defeat, but God does not have our perspective and therefore never accepts defeat.

In that situation, the Israelites would not have accepted defeat if they had changed their perspective from one of looking around and forward to one of looking back. It would have served them well to look back to remember God's previous demonstrations of faithfulness where He, refusing to accept defeat, had delivered them from impossible situations in the past. Then they would not have accepted defeat in their present, causing them to grumble against God in disbelief of His ability to deliver them from this impossible situation. Herein lies the great sin they committed against God, the sin of doubting His goodness, His wisdom and His power. They should have trusted God's goodness rather than accusing Him of bringing them out of Egypt just to die in the desert. They should have trusted that God in His goodness knew of their needs, and that same goodness of God would cause Him to meet their needs.

They should have trusted the wisdom of God in bringing them to the desert rather than complaining that it would have been better if God had left them in Egypt where they had plenty to eat and drink. They should have trusted that the same wisdom of God that delivered their forefathers from the great famine through Joseph's leadership would also deliver them from this famine in the desert through Moses' leadership. They should have trusted that the wisdom of God that brought them to the desert would know how to get them through the desert. They should have trusted that the same power of God that delivered them from the Egyptians with a mighty hand and an outstretched arm through plagues and divided seas would now also be able to provide for their needs and deliver them in this desert.

He brings us to the deserts for the same reasons He brought Lazarus to the tomb—because He loves us and because He desires, for our greater good and His glory, to show us something new about Himself.

In the same way, we should remember God's faithfulness and power and wisdom and love when we encounter our own deserts, so that we never accept defeat. We should never accept defeat, because no matter how desolate, no matter how desperate, no matter how dead our situation might appear to be, God is good, God is wise, and God is able!

God does not bring us to the deserts of our lives to leave us fallen or leave us to die. He brings us to the deserts for the same reasons He brought Lazarus to the tomb—because He loves us and because He desires, for our greater good and His glory, to show us something new about Himself. In the midst of those deserts, we, like Mary and Martha and the children of Israel, might not be able to see how He could be loving us, or understand what His greater good could possibly be, or imagine how He could ever turn this situation around to bring glory to Himself, or know what He is trying to show us or teach us, or even see where His hand is leading us in all of this. Yet in the midst of this desert, in the midst of this unknown, He bids us believe that He is the resurrection and the life and that He will never leave us or forsake us.

As the grave swallows us whole, He asks, “Do you believe this?” While the night of death blinds our eyes, He asks, “Do you believe this ?” As we are wrapped in burial clothing, He asks, “Do you believe this?” After the tomb has been shut up, He asks, "Do you believe this?” After decay has already started to set in, He asks, “Do you believe this?” While everyone else mourns, He asks, “Do you believe this?” After several days have passed without food or water, He asks, “Do you believe this?” When we don’t see any hope, He asks, “Do you believe this?” When we have more problems than resources, He asks, “Do you believe this?”

And in that moment, though all indicators point to the contrary, we must answer as did Martha... with a resounding, unwavering, unfaltering “Yes.” "Yes, I believe. I believe that You in all the fullness of Your goodness, the fullness of Your wisdom, and the fullness of Your power are with me, and You will never leave me fallen. I believe when I am in the presence of my enemies I will fear no evil, for if You in all Your power are with me, who can be against me? You are with me and You will never leave me fallen. I believe that when I have a need and I am in the presence of

the one in whom all the fullness of deity dwells, You, in all Your fullness, are there to meet that need. You are with me and You will never leave me fallen. I believe that when I am weak, then You are strong. You are with me, and You will never leave me fallen. I believe when I don't understand, for then You are wise. You are with me, and You will never leave me fallen. I believe when I walk through the valley of the shadow of death, for there You are the resurrection and the life. You are with me, and You will never leave me fallen. I believe when I am lost, confused, and all hope is quickly dying, for then You are the way and the truth and the life. You are with me, and You will never leave me fallen."

Oh, what resources are readily available when He is with us! Indeed, we shall not want! We know this because the same wisdom of God that devised the plan of salvation through Calvary to meet our greatest need for forgiveness has devised plans for our lives, plans that are good, pleasing, and perfect, plans that give us a future and a hope. We know that the same goodness of God that gave us His only begotten Son to be the sacrifice necessary to meet our eternal need, now gives us all things freely to meet our temporal needs. We know that the same power of God that raised Jesus from the dead is now applied in all of its

exceeding greatness toward us who believe. We know that He who has been faithful in the past is faithful in the present and will be faithful forever in the future. Jesus will never leave us fallen. No matter what situation we find ourselves in, we know that it will not end in death but will be used for God's glory. For our greater good He will call us by name from the tomb of our situation and raise us up from our circumstances to show us something new about Himself and to bring glory to God's only Son, Jesus Christ.

If we believe that Jesus never accepts defeat and Jesus will never leave us fallen, then logically, we should never quit. To be sure, there will be times when we all will want to quit. To be sure, life will try to beat us down. Life will try to beat us down, because we live in a fallen world where we face an ancient foe who, as Martin Luther describes, "seeks to work us woe; his craft and power are great, and armed with cruel hate, on earth is none his equal." This foe seeks to steal, kill, and destroy, but we have a Savior who has overcome, and greater is He that is in you, than he that is in the world. (John 10:10 and 1 John 4:4) Be reminded of Jesus' words:

"In this world you will have trouble. But take heart! I have overcome the world." (John 16:33)

Right now you might be experiencing trouble in this world. You might be experiencing defeat. You might be experiencing the adverse effects of your own past mistakes, character flaws, or poor decisions, but take heart. Do not let yourself be defined by your past mistakes, your present circumstances, or other people's opinions. Let yourself be defined by the possibilities that lie ahead because Jesus has overcome the world.

Note carefully the reason for taking heart. Do not take heart because there are other fish in the sea. Do not take heart because you have another opportunity to try and try again. Do not take heart because you have a positive outlook. Do not take heart because you have spoken your needs to an impersonal universe and are waiting for it to give you what you envision. Those are empty phrases with no substantive basis of truth. Jesus is truth. Jesus is real. Jesus has overcome. Take heart because Jesus has overcome the world. Take heart because Jesus is the Great Warrior. Jesus is the Great Warrior who always places the mission first, the Great Warrior who never quits, the Great Warrior who never

accepts defeat, the Great Warrior who never leaves a fallen comrade, and the Great Warrior who now fights for you. The Bible tells us in Romans 8:37 that because Jesus has overcome, He has made us to be "more than conquerors" through Him.

If you are now down and out because of a persistent character flaw, confess that character flaw, repent, receive God's forgiveness, and take your consequences like an adult. But don't quit! Take heart! Jesus has overcome! If you are losing the battle due to poor choices in the past, learn from your mistakes, pray for wisdom, pray for strength, and believe that God will move on your behalf to redeem your situation. But don't quit. Take heart! Jesus has overcome! If you are innocently suffering at the hands of others' sins, others' poor choices, or others' character flaws, plead your case to the righteous judge of heaven, forgive the other parties, free yourself from bitterness, and believe that God will put your life together again. But don't quit! Take heart! Jesus has overcome!

If you are enduring the discipline of the Lord, thank Him for making you His child, remember that He disciplines you for your good, know that you will share in His holiness, and trust that this discipline will result in the peaceful fruit of righteousness. But don't quit! Take heart! Jesus has overcome! If you have been wounded in battle for righteousness' sake, "Love your enemies, do good to those who hate you, bless those who curse you, pray for those who mistreat you" (Luke 6:27-28), and "Rejoice and be glad, because great is your reward in heaven…" (Matthew 5:12). But don't quit! Take heart! Jesus has overcome! Take heart! "In all things we overwhelmingly conquer through Him who loved us," says Romans 8:37.

Don't quit. Get up. Put the mission first! "Seek first His kingdom and His righteousness, and all these things will be added to you" (Matthew 6:33). His kingdom is the mission; your kingdom is not the mission. Perhaps your present circumstances are God's way of revealing to you that you are seeking your own kingdom first, for your own purposes, rather than seeking His kingdom first. God loves you too much to leave you preoccupied with that which will not satisfy or bring you your greatest joy. Whatever it is you are searching for or hoping to accomplish, it will be added to you only when you put the mission first, only when you seek His kingdom first. Are you seeking love? Peace? Satisfaction? Contentment? Joy? Then seek first His kingdom, and it will be added unto you. Your kingdom

will never provide those things for which you so desperately seek.

One of my favorite verses in the Bible is Jeremiah 2:13, where God says:

> "My people have committed two sins: They have forsaken me, the spring of living water, and have dug their own cisterns, broken cisterns that cannot hold water."

It is one of my favorite verses because of the hope that it gives and because it is the perfect picture of what I have spent my entire life doing—looking to a broken cistern to satisfy my thirst. The hope in that passage lies in its revelation of the source of life-giving water from which we can drink and never thirst again. God Himself is the spring of living water. Jesus told the woman at the well in John 4:14:

> "Everyone who drinks this water will be thirsty again, but whoever drinks the water I give him will never thirst. Indeed, the water I give him will become in him a spring of water welling up to eternal life."

To seek His kingdom first is to drink deeply and freely from the spring of living water, who satisfies the deepest thirstings and longings of your soul. To seek first your own kingdom is to forsake the spring of living water and to drink from a broken cistern, a cistern that cannot hold water. To seek first your kingdom is to expend your life in a futile effort to find happiness, peace, joy, or satisfaction, because your kingdom will not hold water. Your kingdom will not satisfy. Relationships will not satisfy. Success will not satisfy. Power will not satisfy. Pleasure will not satisfy. Comfort will not satisfy. Status will not satisfy. Fame will not satisfy. Wealth will not satisfy. Seeking satisfaction in these things is like going to a bone-dry, broken cistern to satisfy thirst. It will not satisfy. The reason why Mick Jagger can't get no satisfaction is because nothing in this world satisfies. The kingdom of God, however, satisfies: Jesus said that His kingdom is not of this world. If you would be satisfied, put the mission first, seek His kingdom and His righteousness first, and all these things will be added unto you. Seek His righteousness by starting to live as He would have you live. Obey His commands. Surrender to His will. Present your body as a living sacrifice, holy and acceptable unto God. (Romans 12:1) Then you will know that His plan and His will is, "good, pleasing, and perfect."(Romans 12:2)

Stop trying to get God to make your plans come true and start surrendering to His plans for you. His plan for you is to be conformed to the image of His Son. His plan is for your sanctification, which is a fancy word to say that He is trying to make you reflect His holy character, to respond in any situation as He would respond, to act as He would act, to love as He loves, to forgive as He forgives, to love what He loves, to be angry at what makes Him angry, to meet needs as He met needs, to be passionate for that which He is passionate, to seek and to save that which is lost, to be a royal ambassador, to be a member of the royal priesthood, to be holy. When you seek these things first, when you seek His kingdom first, when you seek Him first, then you will find the love, joy, peace, and satisfaction for which you yearn. All these things will be added unto you. You will drink, and your thirst will be quenched.

To seek first your kingdom is to expend your life in a futile effort to find happiness, peace, joy, or satisfaction, because your kingdom will not hold water.

Here is a unique idea. Instead of you defining what it is to have a blessed life and then praying that God would bring that definition to pass, how about giving God a blank check and asking Him to bless you however He sees fit? How about saying to God, "God, I know that You are powerful, wise, and good. So I am trusting Your wisdom to bless me according to Your plans for me, not my plans for me. Lord, like Jabez, I simply ask, 'Oh that You would bless me indeed' (1 Chronicles 4:9 NASB). I believe that because Your wisdom is as high above mine as the heavens are above the earth, I can trust your wisdom to bless me in the greatest possible way, and I also trust your goodness and power to bring about that good on my behalf, showing me something new about Yourself, for my greater good and unto Your greater glory. Whatever you bring in my life, Lord, I just ask that Your hand would be with me, because You are my treasure, my very great reward. There is nothing on earth I desire besides You." How about that prayer?

You pray that prayer and see if God will not come running to your side. See if Jesus, the Great Warrior, will not ride to your rescue, taking up your battle and your fight as His very own.

Can you say that prayer? Can you say that it is God who is your very great reward and not the things that God can give you? While growing up I remember hearing a dear family friend, Gary, recall his wife, Joyce, saying, "Honey, I don't care if we live in a shack, as long as I live with you." For her, any house was a mansion as long as Gary was there.

In Your presence is fullness of joy; at Your right hand there are pleasures forevermore. Psalm 16:11 (NASB)

Could we say that about God? Could we say, "God, I don't care what I go through, as long as I go through it with You, because in Your presence is fullness of joy; at Your right hand there are pleasures forevermore. I'd rather spend one day in Your courts than thousands elsewhere. Come what may, I'm seeking first Your kingdom and Your righteousness, because Your

kingdom is like treasure hidden in a field. I would gladly sell all I have to go and buy that field so that I might have the treasure found therein. I would willingly sell all I have for the treasure of You, because I consider everything else as refuse compared to the surpassing value of knowing You." If you find that you can't say that prayer right now, ask yourself these questions: What is my treasure? Whatever that treasure is, what is it about that treasure that is so enticing? What does my treasure possess that I am so certain will satisfy the needs of my life? In what ways is my treasure so superior to God that makes it worthy of displacing Him as the source of that which I seek? What treasure is more worthy of my love than God? What treasure is greater than God? What treasure is more worthy of my admiration, respect, or awe than God? How can any created treasure be greater than the Creator? What treasure has done more for me, sacrificed more for me, or given more to me than God? Has anyone done more to demonstrate their love for me than God? What more should God be or do to be more worthy of my utmost joy and satisfaction? What is it about me that qualifies me to tell God what He can do to be a more worthy treasure? What are my qualifications? In what qualities do I exceed God to be able to advise Him in ways He can improve to be more worthy of the love and

devotion I now give to another treasure? Do I exceed Him in wisdom? Goodness? Love? Power? Why should God listen to my advice?

If your answers to those questions lead you to believe that God is and should be your ultimate treasure, then you will be able say that prayer and mean it. And then, in time, you will have all things added unto you. You will be more than satisfied. Put the kingdom first, put His righteousness first, and you will be putting the mission first. Put the mission first, and you will never be defeated.

You might not be in a place where you can believe that right now because you feel completely defeated. Perhaps you feel, as the disciples did after the death of Jesus, as though your dreams and hopes have been forever crushed and buried. Life has taken all ambition from you, and you don't know where to go, what to do, or to whom to turn. Perhaps you are on the brink of giving up for good, because there is no other word to describe how you feel than the word defeated.

You feel this way because, frankly, all indicators point to defeat. For you, it might be that the divorce is final. The pink slip just arrived. The retirement account is nearly gone. Your child just left, swearing never to return. A relative mocked your testimony. Your body isn't responding to the treatment. The casket has just been covered with dirt. For the disciples, Jesus was in the grave. Jesus was dead. But Jesus was not defeated. No matter the situation, or how dire the straits, remember, Jesus never accepts defeat.

Jesus never accepts defeat, because in all things He is able to overcome victoriously. Though the divorce is final or another relationship ends in a painful, disappointing breakup, He is able to cause you to rejoice and rest in His perfect, unconditional, and never-ending love. When the pink slip arrives from one job, He is able to cause an offer to come from another job and prove Himself faithful in the mean time. If the child offends and runs away in rebellion, He is able still to touch the hearts of the prodigals, bringing them to their senses, and putting it in their hearts to return home. When the medication fails, He is able to provide the healing balm from Gilead, a balm much more potent than any medicine known to man. And if God in His perfect will should decide that now is the appointed time we all must eventually face, He Himself will go with you through the valley of the shadow of death,

bringing you to that better place where you will be forever healed of both sickness and sin.

God is even able to turn that most final event, the event of placing the casket in the ground, into an occasion of triumph over death by causing new spiritual life to spring forth in the lives of the walking dead, who, after hearing the Christian testimony of the deceased and the blessed life that is now theirs in heaven, accept for themselves God's gift of forgiveness and promise of eternal life. In all things He is able to accomplish great victory on your behalf, unto His glory, for your benefit, because He has all power. That inestimable power is commanded and applied by the perfect knowledge He possesses to bring about the best possible solution, at the best possible time, for your greatest possible good. And you can rest assured that He is favorably disposed toward employing all of His power and knowledge for your greatest good, because He has already demonstrated His love for you in sending His Son to meet your greatest need.

The point of going into such great detail about how Jesus is the only way to salvation is to reveal how hopeless we were and how desperate was our situation without Him. Apart from Christ, we were utterly doomed to an eternal existence of misery and suffering, experiencing forever the unending wrath and fury of an omnipotent deity with no hope for escape or redemption. Yet now we are not without hope because Jesus, moved by compassion, stepped down from glory into our world to provide a way of escape for us, meeting our greatest need at His greatest expense. If the love of Jesus is such that He was willing to go to battle for your eternal salvation, a battle that cost Him everything, how much more willing is He now to fight on your behalf to meet your temporal needs, needs that do not even begin to strain His limitless resources? Jesus did not go to the cross to die on your behalf and secure your victory over death just to leave you defeated in life!

No! Now you are His mission. The Bible tells us that:

> He who began a good work in you will carry it on to completion until the day of Christ Jesus. (Philippians 1:6)

> For those God foreknew he also predestined to be conformed to the likeness of his Son, that he might be the firstborn among many brothers. And those he predestined, he also called; those

he called, he also justified; those he justified, he also glorified. (Romans 8:29)

What, then, shall we say in response to this? If God is for us, who can be against us? (Romans 8:31)

He will keep you strong to the end, so that you will be blameless on the day of our Lord Jesus Christ. God, who has called you into fellowship with his Son Jesus Christ our Lord, is faithful. (1 Corinthians 1:8-9)

Now the God of peace, that brought again from the dead our Lord Jesus, that great shepherd of the sheep, through the blood of the everlasting covenant, Make you perfect in every good work to do his will, working in you that which is well-pleasing in his sight, through Jesus Christ; to whom be glory for ever and ever. Amen. (Hebrews 13:20-21)

Jesus, the Mighty Warrior, is now on mission to complete the good work that He has started in you and He will be faithful to complete it to the very end. His mission is to conform you to His image, to make you perfect in every good work, to do His will to the praise and glory and honor of Jesus Christ. Jesus still places this mission first. If Jesus is for you in this mission, no one can defeat you!

Though no one can ultimately defeat you, there will be times on this mission with God that you will stumble and fall. You will stumble and fall often. If it were up to you and me to complete the mission, we would each and every one fail. But notice who carries it on. It is not up to you or me to carry it to completion; it is God who has the responsibility for carrying it to completion. It is He who keeps us strong to the end, making us blameless on the day of our Lord Jesus Christ. Though you might grow weak and weary along the way so that in a moment you stumble and fall, rest assured that Jesus never leaves a fallen comrade. He will not leave you or forsake you, but rather He will call you, carry you, justify you, and make you perfect through His work on the cross.

His work on that cross has been forever memorialized by the scars on His feet, the scars on His side, the scars on His hands, and the scars on His head. Those scars are an eternal reminder of the horrors of Calvary and the consequences of sin. But at the same time,

they are objects of the greatest beauty in that they proclaim, in a language greater than words, that the price has been paid and the work of redemption has been finished. At times your conscience may plague you with the guilt of your habitual sins so that you hang your head in shame, knowing that you are unworthy to be called a child of the living God. Often the enemy will attempt to condemn you by bringing up those acts of disobedience you have committed in days past, causing you to question your own faith, doubt your own salvation, or believe that your current struggle will end in defeat, all because of your inability to overcome the habitual sins that beset you.

We know with all certainty that the act Satan performs on the stage of our conscience, he takes on the road to the very throne of God where he stands to accuse us before the Father and the Son. And while that great deceiver spews forth his charges against us saints with great fervor and vehemence, I can imagine the Father turning to Jesus seated at His right hand—who, in the midst of all manner of accusations being leveled against the elect, slowly raises His wounded hand in a simultaneous gesture of intercession before the Father and victory over the enemy, who, at the site of those nail-scarred hands, must now stand in silence. And

though those wounded hands say all that needs to be said and are the only defense His blood-bought children need, just to add insult to injury I can imagine Jesus, with a voice that thunders with the sound of mighty rushing waters, saying “Satan, tell it to the hand!”

Now Satan is the one who must hang his head in defeat, because in that moment those scars of battle instantly become badges of honor, bearing testimony to Jesus’ victory on Calvary. He must stand in silence because those scars on the hands of Jesus serve as an eternal reminder that regardless of what has occurred, regardless of what we have done, regardless of how we have failed our sins have been paid for and victory has been won so that the father of all lies now has nothing more to say.

Oh, listen, my friend, though our sins are as scarlet, His blood washes them white as snow. Though our sins are many, His grace is sufficient. We can rejoice with the apostle Paul, who said:

> Therefore, there is now no condemnation for those who are in Christ Jesus. (Romans 8:1)

Each time we come to the Father seeking His forgiveness, we have the intercession of scars that deafen the ears of the Holy One to Satan's charges, drowning out the deceiver's accusations against us. For all eternity, they shout out over and over and over the glorious statement, "It is finished! It is finished! It is finished!" Oh, what joy it will be to one day bow at the feet of Jesus and kiss those scars that so effectively plead forgiveness on our behalf. How sweet it will be to embrace the one who didn't leave us fallen, the one who always placed the mission of our redemption first, the one who never accepted defeat for us, and the one who never quit on us.

The fact that Jesus never quit is a source of great comfort to us when we are tempted to quit due to constant failures along the journey of our mission. If you have often struggled with sin, temptation, failure, or depression, you might think that you are beyond redemption. You might think that you are beyond saving. But to that I repeat, "If there was ever a time Jesus was going to quit on you, He would have quit on you on the cross. But Jesus didn't quit on you at Calvary, and He's not going to quit on you now!"

Your world right now might be like mine was that first Sunday morning at boot camp, standing outside the drill hall waiting to go to Sunday school. The air was bitter cold, the ground was frozen solid, and the trees were lifeless and barren. All of the earth was firmly held in winter's death grip with no signs of its abating. But just above the horizon, standing in stark contrast to the despair of winter, the sun was rising, shining brightly in the sky, holding forth the promise that life would soon spring forth anew. So too, your world right now might be a bitter, cold place, the dead, frozen ground of your circumstances refusing to yield any favorable fruit. Everywhere you look you see shadows of barren trees, mere skeletons of the abundance you once knew or hoped to one day have. Everywhere you look you see nothing but death, disappointment, and despair.

In that moment of despair, I ask you to simply lift your eyes to the heavens, where you will see the risen Son shining brightly in glory. Even now the warm, life-giving rays of His love are bathing your barren land, thawing the frozen tundra of your heart and circumstances in preparation for that soon-coming day when a new, beautiful, fruitful life will bloom.

That is why Jesus came, to give us life, to make our joy complete, and to bring forth much fruit in our lives to His glory. Do not be like the disciples and mourn the winter of your lives as though the spring of new life was never going to come.

Even now, though you might find yourself lying at the bottom of the sea of your life, having been sucked down by the tide of circumstances to such depths that you can't bear the thought of looking up to where you have fallen from because the pain is too great—even though you now may want nothing more than to close your eyes and shut out the visions of pain and loss that surround you, open them. You must open them. Open them to look above your circumstances, to fix your eyes upon the risen Son. Open your eyes to fix them upon Jesus, the author and perfecter of your faith (Hebrews 12:2).

Chapter 6: What You Must Do to Secure Victory

This you must do on a daily basis: you must concentrate on the object of your faith to keep from losing that faith, to keep from losing your way. I learned this one summer afternoon on a road trip from Kansas to Texas. After traveling across Kansas for several lonely hours in a car with no radio, I began to suffer from a case of severe boredom. That was all about to change, as off in the distance, across the wide-open plains, I saw storm clouds gathering on the horizon. It was to be the kind of storm Kansas is famous for. The picture of the sky that day is as clear to me in my mind now as it was when I saw it. The sun, in its vain

attempt to keep from being swallowed by that most severe storm front, not wanting to be robbed of its rightful time to shine, focused all of its intensity on the tips of those clouds, causing the most brilliant silver lining to streak clear across the sky.

The white tips of those ominous, billowing clouds reflected the sun's rays in such blinding splendor that I could not bear to keep my gaze upon them. I was forced to avert my eyes from the tips of those pure white clouds high in the sky down to the point where those same clouds touched the very end of the road I was traveling. At that point, they had changed from a spectacularly bleached cotton white to the darkest charcoal gray, revealing their true nature. I chuckled as I said out loud, "Every silver lining has a storm cloud." This storm, however, was not nearly as potentially treacherous as the foolish actions I next undertook. Insert disclaimer here: DO NOT, UNDER ANY CIRCUMSTANCES, ATTEMPT WHAT I AM ABOUT TO DESCRIBE. THIS STUNT WAS PERFORMED BY A TRAINED, PROFESSIONAL IDIOT!

You know the moment when it begins to rain and those first few raindrops fall on your windshield in just enough quantity to splatter the film of dust and dirt all over the glass, but not in enough quantity to turn on the windshield wipers, because doing so would only spread this opaque mixture of dust and water across the entire windshield, making it completely impossible to see? At this point, most people would simply wash off the muck with windshield-wiper fluid and then turn on the wipers. My car didn't have a radio. Do you think it would've had windshield-wiper fluid?

It was in this moment of windshield-wiper purgatory that I was struck with a flash of brilliance. I decided it would be fun to see how long I could drive through this storm without turning on the wipers. I ask you to refer once again to the aforementioned disclaimer! At first, it was not too challenging, but as the storm intensified, I found it increasingly difficult to see. Surprise, surprise. The more the glass on my windshield was covered with raindrops, the greater effort it took for me to look beyond the raindrops to keep my focus on the bigger picture. I discovered that therein lay the key to making it through the storm—looking beyond the raindrops. I found that it was easier to concentrate on the drops of water pouring down on my windshield than it was to concentrate on the bigger picture.

As I focused on the raindrops my vision would become completely obscured. All I could see were raindrops. Because of my focus on the raindrops, I would lose sight of the signs along the road giving me direction, I would lose sight of my surroundings, and most importantly, I would lose sight of the very road itself. If there had been any cars on the road at the time (WHICH TO THIS DAY I MAINTAIN THERE WERE NOT!), I would have lost sight of them as well. I was at very great risk of losing my way, my sense of direction, getting off track, and yes, losing my very life, all because I was focusing on the raindrops. When I felt this risk rising to levels I could no longer tolerate (a form of solitaire chicken), I would blink, refocus my eyes, look past the raindrops, and once again regain sight of the bigger picture. In an instant, though the sight was blurry, I could again see the road, the signs, and my surroundings. In short, I rediscovered my way. It was all a matter of perspective. The raindrops were nothing more than what I made them out to be. I could make them all-consuming, overwhelming, and vision-blocking, or I could make them out to be what they really were, small drops of water against the backdrop of the bigger picture. I could make them so simply by adjusting my focus.

This is what Paul meant when he wrote in 2 Corinthians 4:16-18:

> Therefore we do not lose heart. Though outwardly we are wasting away, yet inwardly we are being renewed day by day. For our light and momentary troubles are achieving for us an eternal glory that far outweighs them all. So we fix our eyes not on what is seen, but on what is unseen. For what is seen is temporary, but what is unseen is eternal.

The secret to not losing heart in the struggle, the key to not quitting the mission, the principal means of daily, inward renewal, is to fix your eyes not on what is seen but on what is unseen. The secret is to look beyond the raindrops. This is how Paul was able to call his troubles "light and momentary." When I think of light and momentary troubles, I think of bad-hair days, getting barbecue sauce on my tie, getting to church and realizing that I have put on one blue sock and one black sock. But when Paul refers to light and momentary troubles, he is talking about nakedness, exposure to cold, rain, heat, the elements, starvation, shipwreck, multiple beatings and whippings, and on one occasion being left for dead after a stoning. I don't know about you, but I would not put those troubles into the "light and momentary" category. Yet Paul was able to do so, because Paul fixed his eyes not on the temporary raindrops on the windshield of his life, which could be seen, but on the bigger picture of eternity, which could not be seen. That is how he was able to see his problems—not as overwhelming drops of water, causing him to lose his sense of direction, purpose, hope, or joy—but for what they really were, light and momentary troubles that were achieving for him an eternal glory that far outweighed them all.

This was not mere academics for Paul but a principle he practiced every day. This can be seen most clearly when Paul and Silas were put in prison. Read the following story found in Acts 16:23-26.

> After they had been severely flogged, they were thrown into prison, and the jailer was commanded to guard them carefully. Upon receiving such orders, he put them in the inner cell and fastened their feet in the stocks. About midnight Paul and Silas were praying and singing hymns to God, and the other prisoners were listening to them.

Paul and Silas were stripped, flogged, beaten mercilessly, and placed in stocks in a cold, damp dungeon. Yet at midnight, they began to pray and sing. No one else in the prison was singing. What was so different about Paul and Silas? Were they singing because their accommodations were so much nicer than those of all the other prisoners? Were they singing because they had received special VIP privileges that were denied to all the other inmates? Or were they singing because they had a perspective that no one else in the prison had? It was because of their perspective that they did not mourn for the midnight in which they found themselves, but rather they rejoiced over the morning they knew God would surely bring to pass. They did not sulk over the struggles they were enduring, but they sang for the eternal reward those struggles were securing for them.

Perspective is what will keep you from losing heart as well. Perspective is what will renew you inwardly day by day. Perspective will give you the ability to see that your troubles are achieving for you an eternal glory that will far outweigh them all. Perspective is what will cause you too to rejoice in the darkest times of your life. An interesting thing occurred as Paul and Silas

were singing and praying at midnight...they were set free. Read what happened:

> Suddenly there was such a violent earthquake that the foundations of the prison were shaken. At once all the prison doors flew open, and everybody's chains came loose. (Acts 16:26)

Learning to look with an eternal perspective, past your troubles, to see what those troubles are achieving for you, will be what enables you to make it through the storms of your life and will be what gives you a song of praise on your lips in the midnights of your journey. When you can learn to sing by faith in the night, when you can learn to sing in chains, then you too will learn what it is to be set free by the hope of the morning that God will bring to pass. The chains of your struggles may not immediately fall as they did that evening for Paul and Silas. The prison doors of your circumstances may not swing open as quickly as they did for Paul and Silas. In that moment remember one thing, Paul and Silas were free long before their chains fell. They were liberated long before their prison doors flew open. For there was not a prison on earth that could confine their hearts, nor was there a cell in existence that could constrain their worship, preventing their spirits from soaring with the high praises of God on their lips. Stocks were never constructed that could contain the hope of the victory they knew by faith God would one day secure for them!

If you can claim the same promises Paul and Silas claimed, then you can sing the same praises Paul and Silas sang. Perhaps in the depths of that dungeon that night, the verse from Deuteronomy 31:8 came to their minds and inspired the joy in their hearts:

> The Lord himself goes before you and will be with you; he will never leave you nor forsake you. Do not be afraid; do not be discouraged.

Let me add a little something to this verse:

> The Lord Himself goes before you (He always places the mission first) and will be with you (He never quits); He will never leave you (He never leaves a fallen comrade) nor forsake you (He never accepts defeat). (So) Do not be afraid; (And) do not be discouraged."

For as long as these words are true, there is reason to sing. Circumstances will change, but our reason for singing never changes. What God promised in the Old Testament, Jesus performed in the New Testament, for you to be a living testament, a living testament to the prisoners of this world, a living testament to the fact that there is a God in heaven who saves, heals, restores, and renews. It is during the darkest times of your life that you have the opportunity to shine the brightest, making the biggest difference in the lives of others. The enemy intended to use the beatings and imprisonment of Paul and Silas to defeat the spreading of the gospel, to keep people from coming to know the truth. But never accepting defeat, God turned the imprisonment of Paul and Silas into a great victory as all the prisoners witnessed the power of God. The jailer and all of his family became believers.

No matter what your tragedy or trial, look past it, keeping your eyes focused on Jesus, the author and perfecter of our faith. Do not be afraid, and do not be discouraged, for the Lord Himself goes before you, is with you, will never leave you, and will never forsake you. Jesus always places the mission of keeping you to the glory of God first, Jesus will never leave you fallen, Jesus will never quit you, and Jesus will never accept defeat for you. He will, in His perfect way and in His perfect timing, turn your tragedy into triumph!

Epilogue

Let me summarize what my experiences have taught me concerning the shores of the ideal. I opened the book questioning whether we shared the same experience in our pursuit of the ideal: an attractive and happy family life, good health, positive self-image, job satisfaction, financial security, and social status. I used the analogy of straining at the oars in a boat over the rough seas of life, seas that seem to work against us, to keep us from reaching those shores of the ideal.

That analogy reminds me of a story in the gospels, the story of Jesus and the disciples crossing the Sea of Galilee. In the midst of their journey, a great storm

came upon them quickly and unexpectedly. As the waves swept over the small boat, the disciples feared for their very lives. In great panic, they woke Jesus, asking whether He cared if they perished or not, to which Jesus simply and calmly replied, "Peace, be still" (Mark 4:39 KJV). And with that, all was made calm.

My journey has taught me to evaluate what exactly makes up the "ideal" existence and whether or not I should ever strain so desperately or ever be in such a panic to even get to those shores. I began to realize that I was not really after an attractive, happy family life, or good health, or positive self-image, or job satisfaction, or financial security. What I was really after was the peace and contentment I thought all of those things would bring. Those things were simply a means to the greater end, the end of peace—peace being a cessation of wanting and longing, a sense of satisfaction, happiness, purpose, and contentment in life.

I learned that the peace I was seeking could not be found on any shore. I learned that if I opened my heart, looking through the eyes of faith, what I was searching for was right there with me in the boat all along. Jesus.

If I, like the disciples, would just go to Him, He would speak peace to the troubled seas of my heart, giving me the happiness I so desperately sought. I learned He is my treasure, my very great reward. I learned He is the end. I learned that the joy, peace, and satisfaction He gives can be enjoyed here, now, in the boat, on the journey, and not something to be experienced only after reaching some ideal destination. More importantly, the joy in Him on the journey is greater than any joy the destinations of this world can offer. His joy and peace releases me from the prison of circumstances.

That is not to say that I never experience sadness, disappointment, heartache, loneliness, insecurity, or discontentment. But it does mean that I am free from their control. I can acknowledge those realities in my life while rejoicing in the hope that I have in Christ.

I have experienced almost every trial mentioned in this book. But by far, the most painful has been losing my kids in divorce. I never feel more inept as when I try to express the sadness I feel every time I say goodbye to my children. I suffer the grief of death every time they leave me. Nothing in this life wrenches my heart more than knowing I'm missing out on the joys of their childhood. My prayer is to one day live close by them so I can be a bigger part of their lives.

I wrote a tuneless song in the darkest midnight of my life that expresses hope and joy in the midst of this great sadness. It illustrates the tension between acknowledging the pain of this world while rejoicing in the promises of God. I would like to share that song with you in hopes that you might receive the same comfort with which I have been comforted.

Here is how I acknowledge my pain, yet rejoice in the hope Christ has given.

> Nothing breaks my heart or makes me more sad,
> Than the thought of you calling someone else dad.
> Now I'm not sure just who or what I am,
> Till Friday night when I see you three come in.
> For the next two days the world seems right,
> 'Cause then I am your daddy again.
>
> Nothing's right about this, it's all so very wrong.
> My days are 48 hours but my nights are two weeks long.
> I pray to make it through those nights, till Friday night that's when

For the next two days the world seems right, 'Cause then I am your daddy again.

Now I spend my time just thinking of the things I wish I could be…
Like the blanket that you sleep with or the band-aid on your knee,
To comfort you each night, take the pain away.
What I wouldn't give or be to have you here with me.
Although I can't be all those things, I know there's one who can.
He'll gladly be all you need, just bow your head and fold your hands.
I pray your always in His care, and trust your lives to Him;
And ask for one more weekend when I can be your Daddy again.

Nothing's right about this, it's all so very wrong.
My days are 48 hours but my nights are two weeks long.
I pray to make it through those nights, till Friday night that's when…
For the next two days the world seems right,
'Cause then I am your daddy again.

Nothing breaks my heart or makes me more sad,
than hearing you call someone else dad.

But I'm glad you have someone doing all the
things I wish I had…
Brushing your hair, playing catch, picking you up
from school,
Holding you close, telling you it'll be all right when
life has been so cruel.
It breaks my heart, to be worlds apart 'till this war
comes to an end.
I pray that God will bring me back, so I can be
your daddy again.

Nothing's right about this, it's all so very wrong.
The sun doesn't shine without you;
just night since I've been gone.
I pray to make it through this night, hope you think
of me now and then…

And know in your heart, that I can't wait
'till I can be your daddy again.

Nothing makes me happier, knowing together we will
stand,
By His grace, around God's throne, holding each
other's hand.
With open arms He'll greet us, "Welcome home dear
children, to your weekend without end.
Separated at Eden. I've loved you so since then

> That I sent My Son to Calvary, as the sacrifice for your sin,
> To bring us together, to live forever…
> So I could be your Daddy again."

Losing my children to divorce has given me a deeper appreciation for the loss God feels being separated from humanity by sin and how the great Father's heart breaks and how intensely He desires to be reconciled to His children. I've gained a deeper passion for His ministry of reconciliation. So I ask: are you one of God's separated children? Will you stand with us, being welcomed by God's grace, around His throne?

God has loved you since before the day you were born. He loves you so much that He sent His Son to suffer the agonies of the cross so you could be reconciled to Him and live forever with Him. Regardless of what has occurred in your past, all that is required to receive this free gift of eternal life is to confess your sin, ask for and accept His forgiveness, and surrender your life to His good, pleasing, and perfect plan for you. That single act is but the start of a new life and a new, most important relationship with God that in one sense is no different from any other relationship. You grow in your relationship with Him by talking to Him (prayer),

listening to Him (reading His Word, the Holy Bible, and hearing His Word preached in a Bible-believing church), and spending time with Him and your new family of believers in the ministry of a local church.

Once you are a part of this new family, in addition to receiving the blessings of God upon your life, the Holy Spirit gives you a spiritual gift to be used for the benefit of humanity. This gift equips you to be a valuable contributor in reconciling the world to God. Could there be a greater purpose? Could there be a grander cause? All of humanity is careening toward that great and fateful day when God will judge whether we are members of His family or whether we are His enemies because we have rejected His offer of forgiveness,

You can be so much more than a hero who merely saves a temporal life; you can be a witness who saves an eternal soul,

choosing to live independently of His will. Those who have been made righteous by faith in Jesus Christ will inherit eternal life. Those who have rejected God and

His Son will receive eternal condemnation. All of us are heading toward this great and fateful day when we will meet our final and eternal end. You can play a vital, crucial role in sharing the good news that brings others to the saving knowledge of the one who can spare them an eternity of God's wrath, granting them instead God's eternal blessing. What purpose could be greater? You can be so much more than a hero who merely saves a temporal life; you can be a witness who saves an eternal soul, simply by sharing the good news of what Jesus has done for the world.

If you would like to be saved from God's eternal wrath, if you would like to receive this gift of eternal life, if you would like to have your sins forgiven, if you would like to have God make something beautiful out of your life —giving your life meaning and purpose—if you would like to experience the incomparable joy of a relationship with God as your heavenly Father, if you would like to finally know what it is to be truly, purely, and unconditionally loved, if you would like to find the satisfaction for which your soul has been thirsting, then express these thoughts to God:

"God Almighty, I confess my many sins against You. I ask for Your forgiveness. I ask that You would accept

the sacrifice of Jesus on the cross as sufficient payment for the judgment my sin deserves. I believe, Jesus, that You are the Son of the living God, that You died for my sins, were buried, and raised to life on the third day. Thank You for going to the cross on my behalf. I receive Your forgiveness and give You my life, surrendered to Your will, to obey Your commands as my Lord and Savior. In Jesus' name I pray. Amen."

If you said that prayer and meant every word...welcome to the family of God. If you said that prayer or have ever said a prayer like that in your past, your sins are forgiven. You will never be alone again. You are now and forevermore His child, entitled to all the privileges and blessings that attend such a noble title, not the least of which is His presence in the midst of the battles of your life. As great as those battles may be, and as great as the multitudes that oppose you may be, these verses will now and forevermore apply to you:

> "Be not afraid nor dismayed by reason of this great multitude; for the battle is not yours, but God's... Ye shall not need to fight in this battle: set yourselves, stand ye still, and see the

salvation of the LORD with you." (2 Chronicles 20:15, 17)

"All this assembly may know that the Lord does not deliver by sword or by spear; for the battle is the Lord's." (1 Samuel 17:47)

"'Not by might nor by power, but by My Spirit,' says the Lord of hosts." (Zechariah 4:6)

"What then shall we say to these things? If God is for us, who is against us?" (Romans 8:31)

"But in all these things we overwhelmingly conquer through Him who loved us." (Romans 8:37)

As that great hymn says, "There's victory in Jesus, my Savior, forever." In whatever battle you find yourself, when you trust Jesus for your eternal salvation, lay down your life in surrender to His good will, keep your eyes focused on Him—the author and perfecter of your faith—and rejoice in the midst of the fight with great praise in complete confidence of your great and certain victory, then in due time, victory will surely be yours. Victory for you is guaranteed, because you have given

the battle of your life over to the one who always places the mission first, the one who never leaves a fallen comrade, the one who never quits, and the one who never accepts defeat. Victory for you is absolute, because you have given the battle for your life over to Jesus—the Greatest Warrior.

About the Author

H.B. Bender currently resides in Dallas, Texas, where he serves as a chaplain in the Texas Army National Guard.

Visit us online!

Visit The Greatest Warrior Blog
It's a forum for you and for your fellow warriors, regardless of what battles you might be fighting
www.thegreatestwarrior.com

Visit the Stallion Cross Website.
Check in for chapter updates, blogs, and news:
www.stallioncrosspublishing.com

www.ingramcontent.com/pod-product-compliance
Lightning Source LLC
LaVergne TN
LVHW011232080426
835509LV00005B/460

* 9 7 8 0 9 8 4 2 5 7 6 0 7 *